HOW TO DITCH YOUR ALLOWANCE AND BE RICHER THAN YOUR PARENTS!

9 wealth building tools to
make a teen rich

Patti J. Handy

ISBN: 0-9824656-0-2
ISBN-13: 9780982465608
Library of Congress Control Number: 2009903047

This book is designed to provide accurate and reliable information in regard to the subject
matter covered. It is sold with the understanding that the author and publisher, through this
book, is not engaged in legal, accounting, financial, or other professional services. Laws and
practices often vary from state to state, and if legal, financial, or other expert assistance is
required, the services of a professional should be sought. The author and publisher specifically
disclaim any liability that is incurred from the use or application of the contents of this book.

This book is available at quantity discounts for bulk purchases.
For information, email us at patti@kidscashcoach.com.

Gain access to free weekly money tips from Patti Handy
at www.kidscashcoach.com.To get her personal response to your money questions visit her
website and sign up for The Money Minute. Then email her at patti@kidscashcoach.com and
watch for her video response.

Visit www.amazon.com and www.teenscashcoach.com to order additional copies.

Patti J. Handy

Dedication

To my Blake: there isn't anything I wouldn't do for you. You are my inspiration, my motivation, and the glue that keeps me together. If I do nothing more than keep you healthy, happy, and God-centered and teach you how to find peace and prosperity in your life, than I have fulfilled my deepest desire.

I would love to help other parents do the same for their little angels. I have been searching for some time now for some way that I can touch the world in a positive way. I have struggled with the inner mind game that I play with myself. I felt that if I focused on reaching the world, building a business, and creating a legacy, I would somehow compromise my time as a mommy. I would never allow anything to get in the way of my mommy hood, so the legacy never came. Until now.

This book is dedicated to you. It is written for you, yet it is also written for all the parents who want to teach their kids these skills that I will be sharing with you. Specifically, money skills. Now, let me start by saying something very important. When I speak of money skills, my motivation is not to teach you how to be the next multimillionaire that focuses on material wealth. This isn't about showing you how to buy the toys that will bring you happiness. Toys, by themselves, will not bring you happiness. Temporarily, they may, but not for long. Too many people today are focused on acquiring material things, to prove to the neighbors, who they don't particularly care for, that they "made it." Please don't concern yourself with the neighbors, or anyone else's thoughts of you. Your identity, your self-worth and your gift to the world is who you are, not what you have. You are an amazing person, with a gift of compassion, love, sensitivity, and generosity. You already have wealth, my angel. The important kind.

Having said that, learning how to make, manage, and respect your money will have a large impact on the quality of the life you lead. If you fail to respect, save, invest, and, most importantly, share your money, you will struggle most of your life. Money, or the lack of it, will play a vital role in your life.

This book is going to teach you all about money. How to save it, how to invest it, how to manage it. I will show you how to balance your checkbook, deal with credit cards, and even how to buy a house someday. (Okay, maybe we'll start with buying your car.) But those items require good credit scores, so I'll tell you what those are and how to get high scores. Credit scores are even something that potential employers will look at when deciding whether to hire you. I'm going to teach you how to track your spending habits, watch your expenses, and not get into debt. (Debt is sure-fire way to land in stressville.) We will talk about a budget, although I prefer to use the phrase "spending plan." Budget, like the word diet, implies a serious sacrifice. I'll introduce you to the stock market and show you how to invest in mutual funds. The option market that you see me investing in will have to wait until you're older. My hope for you, besides the obvious things of health, peace, and happiness, is freedom. Financial freedom. The freedom to enjoy your life, give back to the world and leave *your* children with this same wisdom. (You better take good care of my grandchildren, mister.)

All of these lessons are being taught to you now. Every day we discuss some form of this information, but I wanted to put it in book form for your future reference. Also, as I mentioned earlier, I wanted to share this with the world as well. For that matter, give this book to my grandkids. The fundamental rules will be the same.

Although managing money is the main focus of this book, I'm going to discuss faith, gratitude, affirmations, your thoughts and how they affect you, and staying centered. All of these attributes are the foundation for your lifestyle habits and happiness. And in turn, believe it or not, your money—how you attract it, how you save it, how you manage it, and how you share it. It comes down to your attitude, gratitude, and lifestyle habits.

So, my angel, enjoy this book and share it with others. I pray that as a result of this book, you are able to enjoy your life, find inner peace, and share your gift to the world. Because, baby, you are the gift of a lifetime!

Table of Contents

Foreword

When I first started my journey in writing this book, the intention was to give my son the money smarts and skills I knew he would need in life. Second to keeping my son healthy, safe and happy, I wanted to prepare him for a joyful and prosperous life.

I would involve him, almost every day, in conversations on spending, saving, preventing debt, creating wealth, thinking in entrepreneurial terms, the stock market, and much more. (Not all on the same day) Some days he would engage wonderfully in the conversation, some days I would get the "deer in the headlights" look. I wanted so desperately to give him everything he would need to enjoy abundance, minimize financial challenges, and live a debt-free life. I wanted to teach him the importance of giving back and sharing his wealth on all levels, not just financially.

So, this book was born. I wrote this book *to him,* so you will find it is very *conversational* in nature. It's a mom talking to her son. I wrote it so he could enjoy it today and reference it tomorrow. There are some topics that are more applicable to him as a teen and some topics for later, such as buying his first home. I wanted it to be as comprehensive as possible without fire-hosing him, so I chose nine of the most important subjects that I think he needs to understand. As I poured out my heart and knowledge (both from my extensive work experience, but more importantly, my life experiences), I soon realized that every parent on the planet would love to give their child this information.

My hope is that this book will give your kids the critical life skill of managing their money. This includes healthy spending and saving habits, understanding credit cards and credit scores, getting a taste of the financial markets, exploring entrepreneurship, and the mindset necessary for success. If they apply this information, they will be well on their way to a prosperous life, living in abundance and financial freedom. This is for my baby—and yours.

Acknowledgements

I'm not even sure where to begin. My heart fills with such joy and warmth when I reflect on the people in my life who made this book possible.

My sweet son, Blake. Thank you for being my inspiration, my motivation, my angel from God. Thank you for being patient while I wrote this book, making dinner when I couldn't, making me laugh when I needed it most, and giving me the most perfectly timed hugs and kisses. Your compassion for others, your generous heart, and your sense of humor are just a few traits that make you so unbelievably special and unique. A teacher once told me, "Blake will make an amazing husband someday." I have no doubt. I love you beyond words, baby.

To say my mom and dad, Roland and Lorraine Handy, have been instrumental would be an understatement. They taught me, at a very young age, how to respect, manage, and make money. I remember my mom and me driving around neighborhoods, just checking out the real estate. They have both supported me, loved me, and encouraged me in everything I've done. They have devoted their lives to their kids (five of us!) in every aspect. Thank you, Mom and Dad, from the bottom of my heart for helping me, loving me unconditionally, believing in me, and always acting so selflessly. I pray I am half the parent you have been to me. I love you both.

My two sisters, Michelle Bernstorff and Cheryl Cunningham, are far more than my sisters. They are my absolute best friends who have stood by me without fail. They listened endlessly to my struggles, constantly propping me back up. They are my pillars and my joy. They are both a second mom to my son Blake, and, as a single mom, I have been so grateful for the sense of peace they brought to me. Thank you both for always believing in me, hearing me ramble on and on, babysitting on a moment's notice and loving me so. I love you, my sisters, with every fiber.

Michelle's husband, Bruce Bernstorff, and Cheryl's husband, Steve Cunningham, have both been my knights in shining armor. They have been amazing in helping me in so many ways. Not only are they second dads to Blake, but they have come to my rescue on countless occasions, especially helping me with house stuff. Thank you, Steve and Bruce, for always taking such good care of me.

My two brothers, John and Greg Handy, have always loved me and supported me in their special ways.

As a computer genius, my brother John has rescued me from many, many, many computer emergencies. On a moment's notice, he would make the drive to my home and make the nightmare go away. Every family needs a computer genius like him. Thank you, big bro! I love you. When Greg and I get on the phone, our minimum talk time is about two hours. Mind you, he only lives forty-five minutes from me, and we chat about once every other week. We have a wonderful bond that touches me deeply. I love you, Gregory.

My adorable niece, Rebecca Bernstorff, was the artistic talent behind my PowerPoint presentations for my DVD collection. She put in many hours, creating the perfect classroom setting. Thank you, Rebecca, for all your hard work and doing such a great job.

My other nieces and nephews, Devin Cunningham, Nicole Cunningham-Wiese, Heidi Bernstorff, Matthew Handy, and Teresa Handy, have inspired me to reach as many teens as I possibly can. I hope this book helps you all become financially free. I love you all.

Thank you to my dear friends who continually supported me during the writing of this book. A special thank you to Tami Smight, Jane Taylor-Sanford, Peter Mackins and Jann Middo, for being such wonderful cheerleaders. I feel so blessed to be surrounded by such an amazing family and group of dear friends.

Wealth Building Tool #1

The Money Mindset and Other Little Life Lessons

As I begin to write this chapter, the U.S. economy is going through one of the worst times since the Great Depression. Possibly even worse. The housing crisis, the credit crisis, high unemployment, brokerage firms evaporating, huge banks closing—you name it, we've got it. Every conversation, at one point or another, touches on the doom and gloom of our economic conditions. These are very scary times, and most people are affected one way or another. Many are losing their homes, some are losing their jobs, while most are watching their 401(k)s dwindle in the wake of this financial crisis. You may be surrounded by people who have personally experienced this pain and loss. Maybe you have friends or family and have witnessed this firsthand. Needless to say, the mood is somber and fearful.

It makes the timing of this topic even more important. What topic? The topic of your mindset, your beliefs, your attitude, staying positive, and being grateful—having faith that everything happens for a reason and the perfect plan is in place. This is a tall order while you watch the world around you struggle.

Let me start by explaining why this is important. Everything you do in life, whether it pertains to making money, having a relationship, or being successful in your career, is directly affected by your thoughts and belief system. Okay, buddy, before you roll your eyes, read on.

Let me break this down: your mind is both conscious and subconscious. Your conscious mind is the intellectual part that accepts or rejects ideas. It reasons and thinks. It says yes and no. Your conscious mind is your *aware* mind. You know exactly what you are doing. Sort of like when I ask you to do something and you say "no," you are consciously being a snot.

Your subconscious mind cannot chose or reject a thought. It must accept any image and cannot differentiate between that which is real or imagined. The subconscious is truly amazing as it functions in every cell of your body.

You may have heard about the natural laws of the universe. Once such law is "The Law of Perpetual Transmutation," which states, "The images you hold in your mind most often materialize as results in your life." You may have heard about the power of visualization—quieting your mind and seeing yourself doing or accomplishing something, feeling it with every emotion and playing it over and over in your mind. Many athletes use visualization techniques before competing in their sport.

Let me tie all this together.

So what does this conscious and subconscious mind stuff mean anyway? Here, in simple terms, is what happens: as a result of your *thoughts and beliefs*, you have certain *feelings* (emotions), which in turn move you to take certain *actions*, which then give you your *results*. So, if you don't like the results you see, whether it be money, career, relationship or health oriented, change your thoughts. Then take the proper action. (By the way, just thinking happy thoughts won't get the job done. You gotta put in the work).

Now, it's easier said than done to change our thoughts and beliefs. We have been programmed, and changing this requires some rewiring. That's where the subconscious comes in. There are countless books about the power of the mind, how it works, visualization techniques, the power of positive thinking, and the like.

My intention is not to give you the details of how the mind works. I can't do that nearly as well as other experts can. These people have spent decades studying the mind, how the conscious and subconscious work and have a far better understanding than I do. But, I want to tell you, in simple terms, what you need to do to stay in "a good place."

Make sure and read *Think and Grow Rich*, by Napoleon Hill, and *The Power of Your Subconscious Mind*, by Joseph Murphy. Both are great, must-read books.

Some of Mom's suggestions

One of the best ways that I have personally experienced in staying positive is being *consciously grateful*. Make it a daily habit, either first thing in the morning or at bedtime, to take an inventory of all the wonderful things with which you are blessed. Acknowledge everything and everyone, from your health, your family and friends, the love of your pet, the warmth and taste of hot cocoa, to the comfort of your pillow. Don't ever take any of it for granted and be eternally grateful. Thank God, every day, throughout the day, for the little things. Having this mindset, one of gratitude, will shift your focus to what is *right* in your world, rather than what is wrong. I call this a "gratitude adjustment."

I started this chapter by sharing the details of the present day economic situation. Many people are getting caught up in the panic, becoming depressed, and making poor choices as a result. Don't get me wrong, times are tough. Life will throw you curve balls that come in all forms. Whether it is health, financial, relationship, or career oriented, life will test you. Nobody said it was going to be easy. But, how you handle these challenges, by way of your perception and attitude, will make a big difference in the quality of your life.

What I want for you is the mindset and understanding of how to help you through those challenging times. Better yet, have this powerful and positive mindset all the time to maximize your experiences in life. I want you to embrace and enjoy life to the absolute fullest, no matter what is thrown your way. When there is panic and crisis in the world, don't bury your head in the sand—but don't get caught up in all the negative either.

You must stay positive, stay on course and step back for a moment and look at the big picture. Don't let the outside world control you. That noise will distract and confuse you.

Affirmations are another way to stay on track with your mindset. By definition, an affirmation is "something declared to be true, a positive statement or judgment." In simple terms, an affirmation is a statement, spoken in present tense, which is both personal and positive. Here are a few examples:

"Thank you, God, for the many blessing you bring to me daily."

"I am enjoying a beautiful life."

"I am doing what I love to do, while money flows to me."

"I am healthy and strong."

"My family and friends are enjoying abundance."

"I am making a difference in the world, doing what I love."

When you repeat these affirmations, close your eyes and visually see—and feel—what this looks like. Experience it as if it were happening this minute. Let your mind and body fully embrace this moment. Bring your emotions into this experience. This is where the subconscious rewiring takes place. You need to make this a daily habit for positive change to take place. Doing this every once in a while won't cut it. Statistics show that repeating a behavior or thought for twenty-one days will create a new habit.

Look at the world as a place of abundance and prosperity. There is more than enough for everybody to enjoy wealth, abundance and a joyful life. God wants this for you, too.

A few more little life lessons from Mom

Tip 1: Another important point I want to make is that of *taking responsibility*. Meaning, when you do something and it doesn't work, take responsibility and make the necessary changes. Don't blame or waste your time trying to find fault in others. If you've done something, anything, in life that was a mistake, acknowledge it and then change it. Make it right. This can be applied to both your personal life and professional life. (Your future spouse will appreciate me for that recommendation.)

Tip 2: Deepen your faith by growing closer to God. As you deepen your faith, your fears will be lessened. Personally, I feel if we live in fear, we are not living in faith. On the flip side, if we live in faith, we don't live in fear. I understand, firsthand, that fear can creep in on us—we are human after all. But if you can consciously stop yourself when you find your mind growing fearful and come back to a place of faith, you will experience more peace. Please understand that fear is in all of us, and it's okay to be in fear. The important thing is that as you have this fear, you work through it with faith and do whatever you are afraid of anyways.

Tip 3: Be aware of your imperfections. Everyone on this planet has strengths and weaknesses. Nobody is a saint, nobody is perfect. Don't expect that of yourself. Accept and embrace your strengths and weaknesses and be confident in your ability to solve whatever problems that may occur. I have total confidence in you. Remember you are perfect in God's eyes.

Tip 4: Don't forget to dream. Dream big. Let your imagination soar and think about what it is you want to do with your life. Why did God give you the talents and skills you possess? What type of profession would make you incredibly happy, while serving the world? Set some goals for yourself, incorporating your dreams. Make sure and write those goals down on paper. Something shifts when goals come out of your thoughts and gets put to paper.

Tip 5: Stay organized. Keep papers, receipts, contracts, and legal documents in a central location or file. Know where everything is at all times. Staying organized will keep the chaos at bay and keep you in control. Knowing you have a handle on paperwork will bring you a sense of peace with your personal and business matters. Keeping your bills in one location will minimize the chance of missing a payment, too. Getting in this habit at a young age will prove especially helpful as you get older. Especially if you get audited.

You were born a compassionate, sweet hearted, empathetic, and loving person. Please don't let the world's negativity take that away from you. Always stay true to yourself, find joy in the simple things and never lose your sense of humor. I must say, you are one funny person.

Nobody can take away your brilliance, talents, or skills. You should stay focused on your dreams and goals, regardless of the negativity that may surround you. This won't always be easy, but I know you can do it. Be determined, stay faith centered, and know that "all paths lead to your greatest good."

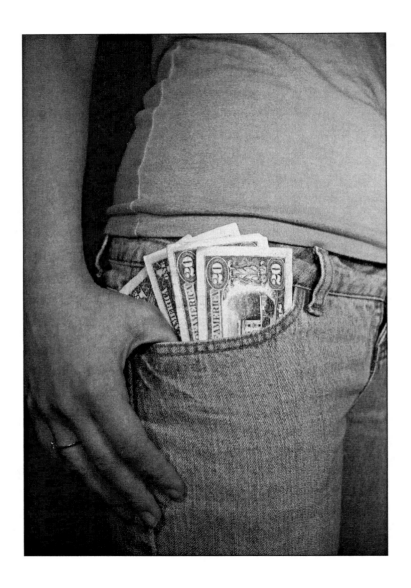

Wealth Building Tool #2

Spend Your Money Wisely

Okay, I can see those eyes rolling. I can hear the groans and moans. But, you have to listen up here! This is important stuff that will impact your life in a big way. So, here's the first secret: There's no magic to creating wealth. Spend less, earn more, and invest wisely. Wow. Powerful huh? Well, I'm sort of kidding, there is much more, but that's the foundation in simple terms.

Here is an interesting little tidbit. In researching the profiles of affluent people, I have discovered there are some common belief systems. First, they live well below their means. What does that mean for you? Well, that means don't spend your money on the latest gadget that you feel you absolutely have to have, when in reality you don't need it at all. It means you don't need the fastest sports car of all time. It means you don't need to buy the latest pair of jeans that everyone loves, especially when they cost $200. Stop trying to impress people with *things*. Before you buy something, ask yourself, "Is this purchase more important than my future financial freedom day?" Wealthy people realize that their financial independence is more important than what people think of them. They realize their social status is second fiddle to their wealth and financial peace.

I understand there is a delicate balance between enjoying your life today and preparing for tomorrow. After all, having millions when you retire won't be exciting if you spent your entire life hoarding your cash. It is very important that you enjoy the journey of your life and treat yourself to those things you deserve. Just remember you deserve to enjoy a peaceful life, not worrying about money, paying your bills and living in lack. It does take discipline. It means creating healthy lifestyle habits, and it means making the right spending decisions. And, yes, it means there will be some sacrifices.

I also understand the peer pressure with which you are faced. I was young once myself. The ironic thing is that some of that peer pressure follows you to adulthood, which is why there are so many people today struggling financially. So, the sooner you learn how to deal with peer pressure, the better off you'll be in dealing with it as an adult. It comes back to what I mentioned earlier: wealthy people realize that their financial peace is more important than other people's opinions. Seriously, is someone else's opinion more important than yours? Especially when it comes to you, your future, and your quality of life?

When I was in high school, one of the things I loved to do was go to the jewelry mart in downtown Los Angeles. I had one friend in particular who loved this same crazy habit. (To this day, we are great friends, albeit wiser.) Now, if you have never been to the jewelry mart in LA, you have to take one trip just for the experience. (I can't believe I just told you to do that—remember it's just for the experience.) It's absolutely amazing. This friend and I loved gold jewelry. I loved necklaces, bracelets, and charms. The charm thing is dating me, but those were the rage back then. Anyway, I'm getting ready to walk out the door, and I said bye to my mom. She then says, "Honey, you should stop wasting your money on gold jewelry. Some day you're going to want to buy a dining room set and won't have the money." I stopped in my tracks and thought to myself, *Are you kidding me?* I said, "Mom, a dining room set? Are you serious? I'm in high school! Now you have me married off, out the door, and shopping for furniture?" I told her I loved her and left for LA—very respectfully, of course.

Fast forward a few years (about five years to be exact), and I'm getting ready to move out and set up house. Dang, I needed a dining room set, along with a bed, couch, some lamps, sheets, towels, kitchen utensils, and some dishes. Guess what? I had the money for all that, plus a nice down payment for my first condo.

Why and how? Well, I enjoyed the occasional trip to LA for some bling, but I also saved. I seriously saved. And I thank my parents for instilling that in me. It's that foundation that allowed me to buy my first place, buy furniture, and withstand the various challenges that came my way.

So, as I said earlier, it's all about balancing and moderation. Enjoy your bling, or whatever your thing is, just be sure to save, too. Funny thing, I rarely wear gold jewelry today.

So, how do you balance that? I do have some suggestions that will put you on the path to spending wisely.

Track, track, track

First, track your spending. How? It's simple! Write down everything you spend during the day—not forever, just for a few weeks, maybe a month. What this does is create a healthy habit of being *aware* of what you spend your money on. Maybe it will make you think twice as well. At the end of the month, add up all those expenditures you made that were not necessary. Maybe it was a coffee, juice, or fast food that you could have grabbed at home. This is the money that you could have saved and not really felt in your day-to-day activities. Eating out is one of the worst ways to "eat" away your money. (Like that pun?) Again, you have to balance enjoying life with planning for your future. I'm not suggesting you never eat out, just watch the little expenditures that you may not think make a big difference. In reality, those dollars add up to big dollars over time. This is a separate step from your checkbook register and balancing your checkbook. (We'll cover that more in detail later.)

Watch the impulse buying. When you see something you want, ask yourself, "Is this a want or a need?" If it is a need, make sure you can pay for it in cash, not by borrowing (credit). (All my gold was bought with cold cash—a scary thing to carry around in downtown Los Angeles. What was I thinking?) Have you met your savings goal for the week? If it is a want, ask yourself why you want it. Is it to impress your friends? Is it something you think is cool? Wait three days and think about it to decide if you really want it. Often, you will realize you don't want it or you would rather spend that money on something else that you want later. If you still want it, make sure it comes out of your play money and not your savings. Have you shopped around for the best price? Being *aware* of this will teach you to be responsible with and to respect your money. Impulse buying will put you into debt, which will create unhealthy spending habits as you grow older. Credit card debt is very expensive and can take years to resolve. Even borrowing money from your parents or friends is considered debt. I'll cover credit card stuff in more detail later. (I can hear you say "yippee" already.)

I recommend you keep a spending tracker in your wallet. It's just a small piece of paper on which you can make quick notes. Here's a sample that you can use. Just copy this and fold it up. If it is easier, track in your cell phone or PDA.

Daily spending tracker...

Date	What bought	How much $$	Why did I buy

It's that simple. As I mentioned earlier, keep this list for a few weeks, possibly a month. This will build your awareness and lifestyle habit of healthy spending. Remember, always ask yourself if the purchase is a *want* or a *need*. Creating this habit now will pay off big time as you grow and start living your life as an adult. Quite frankly, these same habits should continue forever.

The Monthly Spending Tracker

I don't like the word budget, but, I like what the word represents. I know, weird. Let me explain. A budget is like a diet to me. Nobody likes to diet because it implies we need to give something up. Well, we do. We give up the *temporary joy* we experience when we eat something yummy that may not be good for us. But, the rewards and benefits far outweigh what we give up. When we diet, we do so to become healthier, more energized and live a longer, better quality life. We are fit, and we feel better about ourselves, too. So, what's more important? A temporary treat or lifelong health? Same goes for your money. Your budget ("spending plan" is my preferred term) is about watching what you spend and having a plan to secure a better, healthier future. Please keep in mind that I am not saying to live this strict life of only healthy eating and only frugal spending. Life is too short for that. Moderation is key. The goal is *overall good habits* and lifestyle choices.

So, how do we tie all this together? You need to organize your financial commitments and stick to a plan. To help you do this, I put a monthly tracker chart together for you. This plan is assuming you still live at home, without the expense of rent/mortgage and the other expenses that go along with being in your own home (utilities, taxes, home owners insurance, etc.) I'll cover these expenses later when I discuss buying a home.

This tracker (plan) will help you stick with your obligations, put aside money for investing, and keep you on track. It will help you allocate your money and learn to manage it properly. Here's an example: You just got a paycheck for $1,000, and you're thinking, *Yahoo, let's go shopping.* You stop that brain freeze and realize you have financial obligations first. Once you review this tracker, you can determine what you have left over after your commitments are taken care of. *Capiche?*

In the chapter on saving, I'll cover in detail the percentages that should go to savings vs. spending. This will help you determine where your money goes as well. All this information will tie together.

Where oh where has all the money gone...	
Monthly Money Tracker	
(for those who still live at home)	
Income:	
Wages/Salary	_____
Allowance	_____
Other	_____
Expenses:	
Savings	_____
Car payment	_____
Car insurance	_____
Gas-car	_____
Car maintenance	_____
Public transportation	_____
Cell phone	_____
Entertainment	_____
CD's/DVD's	_____
Subscriptions	_____
Clothing	_____
Hair/nails	_____
Gym/Health club	_____
Textbooks	_____
School supplies	_____
Credit card	_____
Gifts	_____
Donations	_____
Food/Drinks	_____
Other	_____

Now, writing out the check

When it's time to actually whip out the checkbook (I use that term "whip" loosely), you have to know how to fill it out correctly. Here is a sample check:

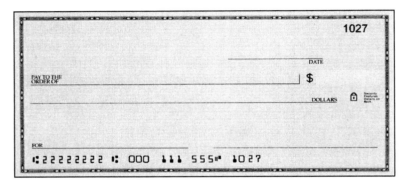

It's actually very simple to complete a check correctly, but when you do it for the first time, it may seem a bit scary—and exciting.

Here are the specific items to enter and how it's done:

- The **date** is the current date. You can either write out the month or just use the number. For example, you can write, January 27, 2009 or 1/27/2009. Either way is fine.
- **Pay to the order of:** The person or company that the check is payable to. Make sure to fill out completely. Don't leave this spot blank or let someone else fill out. If you are at an establishment that has a stamp, you can have them

stamp it. I suggest you watch them stamp it to confirm.

- **Amount $**: This is where you put the amount: dollars and cents in number format. For example, $25.40.
- **Dollars line:** The long line under the "pay to the order" line is where you *write out* the dollar amount you put in the amount box. For example, with the amount above, it would read, "Twenty-five dollars and 40/100-------------." Always draw a line across to the end.
- **Signature:** This is where you sign your name and promise to pay.
- **Memo/For:** This is an optional section for you to fill out. It allows you to make note of what the purchase was for, in case you want to reference it later.

There you go! You're on your way. Remember, just because you have checks, doesn't mean you have the money to use those checks. Balance your checkbook every month and keep a running tally on your balance always.

The checkbook register

So, here's the beautiful thing. Now that you are in the habit of thinking before you spend and documenting your spending, the checkbook register becomes very easy. It's a natural progression and basically a continuation of what you've already been doing—with a couple, easy additions.

Once you are old enough to open a checking account, you are given a book of checks along with a checkbook register. This register is much like the daily tracker you are already using—at least, you better be using!

It is meant to help you know the running balance in your checking account. Basically, every deposit and every withdrawal gets written down, so that at any moment, you know what available balance you have. Failure to do this can be expensive. Let me explain.

Having a checking account is a huge responsibility, and it can cost you dearly if you don't maintain (balance) it every month. If you happen to spend more than what you have, the banks will slap a fee on you that will hurt. It can be in the form of an overdraft or service fee. Paying these fees is no different than you taking a $20 bill and lighting it on fire. Poof, it's gone. Think about how hard you worked for that money and don't let that happen. If you have that kind of money to waste, give it to me. I'll make good use of it.

When you use a debit/check card, it's the same as writing a check. The expense gets deducted from your account immediately and you must write this expenditure down in your checkbook register. (A debit/

check card looks like a credit card, but is very different. Debit cards are like cash. I'll cover credit cards in greater detail later.)

Some banks may also charge you a monthly service fee, phone bank fees, ATM fees, or overdraft protection fees. Make sure you know what these fees are, or better yet, find a bank that waives these fees for teens. Be sure to deduct these fees in your checkbook register, as these can add up and mess up your math.

So, let's talk about balancing your checkbook. Here's the step-by-step process.

First, let me say, it's not that bad. If you keep up with it monthly, it is quite easy. You must do this every month to confirm that neither you nor the bank made an error. (Yes, banks can make errors, too). If you don't check and balance, it can result in an overdrawn account and expensive bank charges. Like I said earlier, you work too hard to let the bank take that money away from you.

Okay, let's start!

Step 1:

Take your checkbook register and bank statement and put them side by side. Go down each check that you wrote (or debit card purchase) and compare that to your bank statement. Put a check by each entry that exists on both the statement and your checkbook register. This basically means that your check "cleared" the bank. Do the same for all of your deposits. Remember to add interest earned to and deduct service charges from your checkbook register. These will appear on your statement.

Now, Step 2 will basically help you compare the two by just adding and subtracting. The most common mistakes are arithmetic, so use a printing calculator to help.

Step 2:

On your bank statement do the following:

Start with: Ending balance from statement $_____

Add: Deposits not on statement $_____

Subtotal = $_____

Subtract: Checks outstanding (did not clear) $_____

BALANCE (this should agree with checkbook) $_____

In your checkbook register do the following:

Start with: Balance from checkbook $_____

Add: Interest earned or other credit shown
on statement, but not in checkbook $_____

Subtotal = $_____

Subtract: Service charges or other debits shown
on statement, but not in checkbook $_____

BALANCE (this should agree with statement) $_____

Step 3:

Be very proud of yourself! This is a huge step towards being responsible and managing your money.

Having said all that about checkbook registers and balancing your checkbook, you do have an alternative. Banking online and various accounting software has made the task of paying bills and balancing your checkbook much easier. Understanding the concepts of maintaining your balances and tracking your spending is still imperative. (This is why I took you through the exercise.) If you decide to bank online and use checks concurrently, be sure to keep your checkbook register updated.

Your lifestyle choices

So, you've learned how to track your spending and balance your checkbook. Awesome. I touched on the topic of lifestyle choices and not being concerned with other's opinions, but I want to go a bit deeper on this subject. I know you will be working hard for your money. (I'm confident you will also be *working smart* for your money). It's so important to enjoy the journey of life, embrace the moments with your family and friends, travel, enjoy a hobby, and just do what makes you happy. It's not all about working and saving. Life is precious and life is short, so I encourage you to take it all in with an open heart.

As I mentioned earlier, it's takes a delicate balance of wisdom to enjoy your life while planning for your future. Without a plan in place, your dreams of financial freedom and financial peace simply won't happen. Keep in mind, I'm not just referring to retirement. Financial freedom happens throughout your life.

Without a plan, a course of action, the goals you set for yourself will not become a reality. Just like a roadmap, or GPS in today's world, we need a starting point and a destination. Once we know where we are going, we then put our plan in place to get there. What's your destination? Where do you want to see yourself? You have to determine that, so the motivation and drive will be focused.

I would love to see you enjoy life to it's fullest, realize your goals and dreams, and live life with no regrets. You are the only one that can make that happen and the only one that has your dreams.

So, having said all that, here's the point that I started with. Your lifestyle choices and habits will greatly affect you realizing your dreams. Here it is in simple terms. Imagine you're out with your friends, and you stop for lunch, juice or a coffee. Let's say that stop costs $4. Harmless enough, right? Wrong. Did you know that if you put $4 a day into an account that earns 10% on average, you would have almost $17,000 in just ten years? Remember that car you want to buy?

You better start saving, because this momma won't be buying it for you. Let's say you do that same $4 a day for 20 years. Well, the magic of compounding interest and time would bring that to almost $61,000. Shocking isn't it?

It's those little choices that you make day to day that add up to big differences in your life. Whether it be a fast-food stop or an impulse purchase, these choices will impact your bottom line faster than you can say, "Mom, can I borrow some money?"

Please understand that I'm not saying you can't ever enjoy a nice meal out with your friends. By all means, go enjoy yourself. Just do it in moderation, just like that diet we spoke of earlier. Don't splurge (binge), because you know what comes next. Although it goes without saying, always use cash (and track, of course) these outings. Do not put on credit.

Some last thoughts regarding spending: As in life, when things are *in order*, meaning organized, there is a tendency to experience more harmony and peace. When there is chaos, there is almost always some type of headache and/or heartache. When it comes to your spending, keep all receipts and bills in an organized file. Know where everything is in case you need it for tax purposes, school purposes, or anything else. Getting in the habit of staying organized will serve you very well as you get older.

This will teach you to stay on top of your paperwork, whether it relates to your personal life or work life. As you get older, you will need to organize your home receipts, investment statements, real estate documentation, insurance information, living trust (getting ahead of myself here—sorry), and much more. I realize that most of this doesn't pertain to you right now, but you get the idea.

So, in the end, enjoy life, spend your money, but do it wisely. Watch the impulse buying, watch the fast food outings, and don't fret about the latest and greatest gizmo to impress your friends. Have fun, but keep your financial freedom destination in mind, too.

Wealth Building Tool #3

Debit and Credit, Just Don't Forget It

"The rich rule over the poor and the borrower is servant to the lender"
Proverbs 22:7

Ahh, that little plastic card. What would life be like without it? I guess it depends on how you use it. This chapter will guide you on how to use credit wisely, explore the pros and cons of credit cards, and tell you how to stay out of hot water.

Let's start by explaining the difference between a credit card and a debit card. Both are plastic little cards that can be swiped to purchase something, but they are very different. Credit accounts typically cannot be opened until you are eighteen years old, but debit cards can be received earlier. Check with your bank or credit union for their minimum age requirements.

Debit cards

A debit card, which is also used as an ATM card, takes money out of your account much like writing a check does. Consider it immediate. The debit card is tied to your checking or savings account, so any activity with your card affects your account balance almost immediately. (By the way, ATM stands for automated teller machine, although *my* personal definition is "Always Takes Money.")

When you purchase something and swipe your debit card, you must *always* write that purchase down just as if you wrote a check. You need to be certain to keep the running balance in your account, because if you overdraft (spend more than you have in the account), you will pay some ugly fees. Some lenders won't approve the transaction if you don't have enough money in the account, while I have seen some lenders allow the transaction but slap you with that fee. Be sure to check with your bank as to their policy, but regardless, always know your present balance. As I've said over and over, you work way too hard to donate money to your bank in fees.

When you need cash out of your account, you would use that debit card at the ATM. Again, make sure you make note of your cash withdrawal in your register. If it's out of your checking account, use the same checkbook register.

I've heard some people say, "Why was I able to make that purchase if I didn't have the money in my account? Why would the bank let that purchase go through?" First, it's your responsibility to manage your money, not the bank's. Second, the bank profits from the fees they charge you. Sorry, they don't give much love in that area. I know you are tired of hearing me say to track your spending, but track your spending.

On to the credit cards

When you use a credit card, think "borrow." If you use a credit card to purchase something and don't pay off the balance in full when your bill arrives, think "bad debt." There, I'm done.

Sorry, I know sarcasm is irritating.

Before I go into details and examples, understand this bottom line: credit cards, if used incorrectly, will wreak havoc on your life. Getting out from credit card debt is very difficult and extremely stressful. Once the snowball starts, it can be quite the challenge to demolish. It can take years and years to pay off credit, which means that $75 pair of jeans or $350 cell phone has cost you hundreds and hundreds of dollars, if not thousands. Ouch.

When you purchase something using a credit card, the charge is not deducted from your checking or savings account like a debit card. With a credit card, your purchases are totaled and you will receive a monthly bill. When that monthly bill lands in your lap, hopefully you aren't surprised with "wow, things sure do add up." My guess is those words will come out of your mouth on a few occasions. I know they have for me. They do for everybody, so don't beat yourself up for it. The important thing is what you do next.

If you pay the bill in full, you generally won't be charged any interest. There shouldn't be any finance charges and if you pay on time, there won't be any late fees. You've been able to "borrow" money without any charges for a short period of time for free. Be careful here though and watch the due date. The billing cycle will vary from card to card, which means if you have more than one card, they will typically be due on different days.

When you receive your bill in the mail, you will be given the option to make a minimum payment. Taking this option is a huge mistake. If there is only one thing you take away from this entire book (which would break my heart), let this be it. *Don't pay just the minimum payment.* If you don't pay the bill in full, you will incur interest charges or finance charges, and, if the bill is paid late, some late fees. If you go over your limit on the card, you will get slapped with an additional fee, too. Yikes. To add salt to the wound, if you go over your limit, many banks will raise the interest rate on your card and you won't be able to lower it again. Talk about a costly mistake! As you fall behind in payments, your credit scores will be hurt in the process, too. The chapter on credit scores will go into this subject in depth.

I'll share some startling numbers with you in a moment—the true cost of an item if put on credit cards and not paid in full.

The nice part

Having said all that, credit card usage, if done correctly, will help you build a credit history, will increase your credit scores, and is quite convenient. There are many pros to having credit cards.

If you are in a pinch or in an emergency situation, a credit card can be a life saver. (I'm not talking about *needing* those new clothes here.) If you need your car towed, run out of gas, have a medical emergency, or any other type of unexpected surprise expense, a credit card is a godsend.

Credit cards are also easier to use when you travel, eliminating the need to carry cash. If cash is stolen, you're done. If your card is stolen, you can get a replacement quickly and not be on the hook for charges that aren't yours. Just be sure to call the credit card company immediately.

Some of Mom's advice

There are some smart ways to use cards and some things to look out for. These tips will guide you along the way.

- When you get your first card, I recommend a low credit limit, such as $300. This means that you aren't able to spend more than $300 on your card before paying some of it down. It acts like a ceiling for you. This way you can learn to manage buying and paying, without the risk of getting too deep. As you become more comfortable with using the card, you can request a higher credit limit. Take that responsibility seriously, as mistakes or misuse can affect your credit history for years. As I've mentioned, your credit history can save you (good credit scores) or cost you dearly (poor credit scores) over time.

- When you are ready for your first card, try to get a VISA, MasterCard, or Discover. The credit bureaus look more favorably on these. I prefer this type of card over department store or gas station cards, as these typically have higher interest rates. You can use the VISA/MasterCard anywhere, including department stores. Sometimes, starting out, it may be hard to get a bank card (VISA/MasterCard), so you need to go the department store route. In that case, get a card from a larger store, not a specialty retailer. I suggest a Sears or JCPenney type store.

- Find a bank that doesn't charge an annual fee. Some banks will charge you an annual fee and some won't. If your bank charges you one, tell them you won't open a card unless they waive that fee, forever. There are plenty of places you can go and get that fee waived. Everything is negotiable.

- Protect yourself by taking a few precautions when using your debit or credit cards. You will be asked to choose a PIN number on your debit card. PIN stands for Personal Identification Number. Be sure to memorize it and don't share with anyone. Pick a number that would be hard to guess, not your birthday or year of birth. Even your phone number or address should be avoided. Don't write this number down and leave in your wallet or in a location that is easily accessible. This PIN number will be asked of you (you will enter on keypad, never give this to employee) when you withdraw cash from an ATM or make a payment with your debit card.

- Make sure to review the charge amount when you are making the purchase and keep your receipts. You will want to cross check the receipts against the credit card bill to be sure there weren't any mistakes. Everyone makes mistakes, so be sure to take the time to check your statements completely. You may even find a charge the bank charged you that shouldn't be there. I've seen that. If this happens, call the bank and get that charge reversed from (taken off of) your bill.

- When shopping for a credit card, be aware of the details: specifically, whether the interest rate is variable or fixed, what the interest rate is, and if they are teasing you with an introductory rate. Obviously, the lower the interest rate, the better. A fair interest rate is between 5% and 11%; anything higher should be avoided. Keep in mind the interest rate only comes into play if you don't pay your credit card in full. If you pay in full every month, the interest rate is not important. But, you should still strive for the lowest rate in case you have to carry a balance for a short time. As with everything, this rate is negotiable. If the credit card company starts to move this rate up on you, get on the phone with them and tell them you will take your business elsewhere unless they work with you. There are some student credit cards out there, with nice benefits and services, so be sure to take the time to do your homework.

- If your bank offers you a credit card with an *introductory rate*, run like the wind. This means they will be nice-nice for one year, then make you cry like a baby. The best case scenario is the lowest *fixed rate* you can find. Avoid variable interest rate cards as well. Make sure to read the fine print so you know what you are getting yourself into. Here again, doing your homework will save you lots of money over time.

What does it really cost you?

As I've mentioned, if you don't pay your credit card off in full every month, you will incur interest expense, possibly finance charges, and, if late, a late fee. For this example, let's just look at the interest expenses.

Okay, say you decided you had to have the latest cell phone. You didn't want to wait until you had the cold hard cash in hand. Let's say that cell phone was $500, and you decided to charge the amount. I'll give you a couple different scenarios of what that cell phone costs you and how long it would take you to pay it off, if you only paid the minimum amount.

Credit card balance	Interest rate	Minimum	Interest cost	Months to pay off
$500	20%	$25	$113	25

In this example, you would have paid $613 for that cell phone, not $500, and it would have taken you over two years to pay it off. My guess is that by that time, a newer phone would have come out. Keep in mind, this does not take into consideration any finance charges or late fees that may have been incurred as well. Ouch.

Let's look at a few more examples:

Credit card balance	Interest rate	Minimum	Interest cost	Months to pay off
$1,000	18%	$50	$198	24
$2,000	18%	$100	$396	24
$2,000	20%	$50	$1,323	67

Did you catch that last one? It would take you almost 5½ years to pay this off and cost you an additional $1,323 by paying the minimum only payment. Talk about crazy! The minimum payment is typically calculated at 5% of outstanding balance (as of this writing), but can differ. The above scenarios are for instructional purposes only.

Here's something very important I want you to remember. We don't necessarily need to go out and buy one large ticket item to bring our credit card debt up. Items add up quickly. One dinner out, one new pair of shoes, a must have pair of jeans, then some coffee stops with friends, a few movies out, some music downloads—you get the picture. A few dollars here and there add up to a boatload of moolah.

If you carry that balance to the next month, then make a few more purchases, suddenly it's very hard to catch up. This is how people get into serious trouble. Once that cycle begins, getting out from underneath credit card debt is very difficult.

This takes us back to something I spoke about earlier and that is being aware when you make purchases. Asking yourself if this item is a *need* or a *want*. Depending upon the item, is it coming out of play money or short-term savings? Are your savings goals being met?

Don't get me wrong here, I don't want to take the wind out of your sails. But, making wise decisions when you are looking to purchase something can save you potentially thousands of dollars over time.

I want to take this one step further and show you some bigger credit card balances. Let's look at a few examples that will scare you enough to make the right choice.

Credit card balance	Interest rate	Minimum	Interest cost	Months to pay off
$5,000	18%	$100	$4,311	94

On this one, the interest alone costs you almost as much as the debt itself and will take you nearly eight years to pay off. Note: *your required minimum payment would probably be higher, but I wanted to illustrate how interest charges accumulate.*

$5,000	18%	$500	$458	11

This shows how a higher monthly payment will reduce your interest expense and time to pay off. If you can't pay in full, make the most payment you possibly can to reduce interest.

I can go on and on with different examples, but I think I've made my point. (Please tell me I have)

There are some great calculators online that will allow you to put in different scenarios. I like www.moneychimp.com, then go to the calculator link. The "debt payoff" option will let you enter various balances, rates and minimum payments. It's fun to play with and it's also a real eye opener.

Please, please, please, only use credit when you know you have the cash to pay it off in full. Think hard before you put anything on credit and don't let yourself get in hot water. Unless, of course, it's a spa.

Wealth Building Tool #4

Good Debt and Bad Debt

Debt is one of those words that generally I don't like. Nobody likes debt. Basically, debt means you owe someone money. It can be a bank, a credit card company, a car finance company, or a friend. (Borrowing money from friends will almost always end up in a disaster—don't do it! I also don't recommend you lend friends money unless you are willing to accept the fact that you probably won't get it back.)

When you borrow money to buy something, you need to pay it back (duh) with interest added on. With some companies, tack on an additional finance charge if you're late. Getting out from under the original borrowed amount can be very costly. If you put those $50 pair of jeans on your credit card and don't pay it in full when the bill arrives, those jeans will cost you a lot more than $50. Depending on your interest rate and how quickly you can pay it off will determine what you really pay for those jeans *you just had to have*. I covered that extensively in the prior chapter.

That kind of debt is what I call bad debt. You bought something, had to pay interest and/or finance charges, and didn't gain anything from it. I know you will argue with me here, because you'll say, "But I just got a cool pair of jeans." Yes, you did. And you may have benefited from it from an emotional perspective. I can't take that away from you. But, how long does that last? A few days? Weeks? Then what? You still have that debt owed and suddenly your jeans are just another pair of pants.

Anything we purchase with credit (borrowed money) and don't receive a *financial benefit* from is considered bad debt. Let's take your car payment for example. You need to drive, which means you need a car. You don't have the cash to purchase a car outright, so you need to borrow (finance) to make the deal happen. The obvious benefit is you now have a car (hopefully one with air bags everywhere possible). You can get to work, school, social events, etc. Those are definitely benefits. But are they financial benefits?

You can argue that going to work generates money, and you need a car to get to work. Going to school, well, that's obvious. Here's where it gets tricky. What kind of car did you buy? Was it the one that was used, a little older perhaps, and very affordable? Or did you *have* to have the new car with those amazing tires and rims, GPS system (although I do love those—saved me many times), and stereo system that makes most people's organs dance in a way that just isn't right?

See where I am going here? We all need to purchase goods and services. But, make wise, careful, thought-out decisions about those purchases. Make sure you shop and compare for the absolute best deal out there. Try to keep the emotional factor out of it. I realize that can be tough, but having that awareness is often all you need. Ask yourself, "What am I giving up by buying this particular item at this particular price at this particular time?" I ask that you *forward think*.

Basically, I am trying to get you to understand that all the choices you make have a price. You obviously need a car, you obviously need clothes, food, etc. When it comes time to make those purchases, especially the bigger ticket items, think hard about what it is you are getting into. Realize that there are consequences to your decisions and actions—good and bad. Try to avoid the emotional "gotta have it now" purchase. I can almost guarantee you that you will look back and wish you hadn't done it.

Here comes the good debt

Now, let's talk good debt. Good debt is debt that you take on that will benefit you financially. Meaning, your money will make you more money. Real estate is a perfect example of this.

In order to buy a home, you need to borrow money from the bank. This is called your mortgage or loan. This is obviously debt. But, with real estate, values will generally appreciate over time. (There are cycles in real estate where values will decline, but real estate should be considered a long-term investment—at least in my book). Over the long term, real estate has historically done well. Although we are presently in a housing crisis, many see this as an amazing opportunity to purchase a home.

This appreciation, or increased equity as it's called, was gained by you simply owning the house. You didn't need *to work* for it. Aside from you maintaining the house or perhaps doing some home improvements, you didn't have to do much. Keep in mind that maintenance costs will vary, depending upon the condition of your home.

A little side thought: Some people will take this increased equity out of their home (by taking a second loan or refinancing) and purchase more real estate. I call that leverage. Think about this. The equity in your home is just sitting there, right? It doesn't earn you interest, and it's not working for you. Your home will appreciate the same amount, whether you use that equity or not.

I'm getting a bit advanced here, but I want to plant the seed for you. Think about using your money to make more money. (I see a second book here.) You must be very careful not to over-extend yourself. This should only be done when you fully understand what you are doing and have done the math. You should also consult a CPA or real estate professional whom you trust.

If this strategy is done correctly, you can actually pay off your home faster, which is the ultimate goal for some people. This topic is way beyond the scope of this book, but I wanted you to have this tidbit of information for the future.

Now, having said that, some wonderful opportunities arise when you are able to purchase a second rental home for investment purposes. Not only do you benefit from the appreciation of that home, you receive rental income (which offsets the mortgage and other expenses), and great tax benefits. Sometimes you actually have a *positive cash flow*, which means your rental income is more than your mortgage payment, property taxes, home owners insurance and all the other expenses you incur when owning that home. Again, I'm getting ahead of myself here, but understand that real estate is good debt.

As you can see, not all debt is bad. If you're ever uncertain, ask yourself this question: "Is this purchase helping me financially?"

Let me close this chapter with one last thought. I realize that life isn't all about making purchases that only benefit us financially. This book represents that. My hope is that you give careful consideration to what and why you buy something, use credit only when absolutely necessary, and do everything possible to pay that credit in full when the bill arrives. I also realize that *life happens*, and this isn't always possible. I get that. But if you have this foundation and understanding in place, you should be able to weather the storms of challenging times. I also want to make it crystal clear that I want you to enjoy life to its fullest, embrace fun times, and give back. Being financially savvy will help you accomplish this.

Wealth Building Tool #5

The Art of Saving

*"In the house of the wise are stores of choice food and
oil, but a foolish man devours all he has"*
Proverbs 21:20

Saving money is somewhat like an art. It requires discipline, focus, determination and a deep desire to create something. What are you creating with savings? Peace of mind. Financial freedom. The ability to make a difference in the world by giving back.

Learning how to save can come easily for some, yet for others it can seem impossible. It comes down to a few simple steps. Let's first take a look at what saving is. Simply put, take the money you have coming in (income) and subtract out the money you have going out (expenses). The difference is your profit, or savings, in your case. (For a business, the term "profit" is used). I have a bit of spin on this though. One of your "expenses" should be "savings." In fact, you should pay yourself first, every single month. More on this later.

Let's take this one step further. The only way to increase the *savings* number is either to *increase* income or *decrease* expenses. It's that simple. I can give you some fancy calculation on how to increase your savings by this or that percentage, but that would just confuse the issue. And for what? The reality is you either need to have more money coming in or less money going out, or both.

Increasing income can happen in various ways, depending upon your age. If you have a job, ask yourself, "Can I do better by working somewhere else?" "Is this company paying me what I am worth?" "What are my options for higher paying jobs?" Better yet, ask yourself, "How can I take what I love to do, utilize my skills and talents, and create my own company?" You may need to start your own company while working a regular job to keep the money coming in. (As you know from a previous chapter, I love the idea of entrepreneurship.)

Decreasing expenses is where you will need to take a hard look at some things. In the spending chapter, I gave you a spending tracker. If used, this will shed some light on where all your money is going. I suggest you look hard at that list and determine where you can shave off some expenses. How much is going to eating out? Coffees? Downloading songs? Remember, every dollar counts! You get the idea.

It comes down to lifestyle habits, and sometimes a lifestyle change has to be made. Your priorities have to be crystal clear. Is your first car or first home more important than eating out? As I've said earlier in the book, this isn't about cutting fun or enjoyment out of life. It's about creating healthy habits and an awareness and a desire for financial independence. Some things just have to be eliminated, at least for now.

It's about balancing. Keep this in mind: as you create these healthy habits at a young age, you will be setting yourself up for an amazing future—one filled with financial peace and abundance. You can dine anywhere you desire and treat your friends if you want. It's about delayed gratification. Realize that you may have to give up something today to have something so much better tomorrow.

Paying yourself first

One expense that should be number one on your list is paying you. That's right. The first payment you make every month is to a savings or investment account in your name. I don't care if its $10, $100, or $1,000 a month, just make it. Get in the habit of paying yourself first, every single month, consistently. You will be shocked at how quickly that adds up. (I'll be giving some examples of the power of compounding interest and time, just hang in there with me.)

I would recommend you have the amount automatically deducted from your checking account and transferred to the savings or investment account you opened for this purpose. Most banks will have this automatic withdrawal feature for you; all you need to do is fill out a form at your bank, or sign up for it online. If this is done automatically, you are less likely to forget, or worse, spend the money on something else.

This one simple tip is something that the wealthy individuals do. They understand the power of compounding interest and the power of time. They also live well below their means, as this savings habit is a priority for them. There is no magic bullet or overnight wealth. (Unless, of course, you win the lottery or inherit some serious cash—neither one I recommend you assume is going to happen.)

Compounding interest and time: your new best friends

This is the part where I have fun. I'm always excited to see people's faces when I give them some hard numbers when it comes to saving money over time. I get everything from shock to laughter. I like them both.

Okay, this is where I show you the power of your little dollars becoming big dollars over time. This will motivate you to think twice when you think to yourself, *Geez, this $4 cup of coffee can't affect me that much.* I gave you some statistics in the spending chapter, but we will expand it further here.

Let's play with some numbers.

Let's assume you've opened up a savings or investment account with $100 to start. You can manage to put an additional $40 per month into the account. That's $10 a week basically. No biggie. You probably wouldn't miss it. If that account was earning you 8% interest, compounded annually, your account balance after five years would be—drum roll please—$3,188.18. Amazing huh? Just $40 a month and a few years later, you have over three thousand bucks.

Now, to show you how the power of time and compound interest work, take that same example just a step further. What if you put that same $40 a month into the same 8% account, only this time left it there for ten years, instead of five years? Another drum roll please—$7,725.73. Seriously, doesn't that blow you away? How about twenty years, just for fun—$24,189. What about forty years? $136,467! Do you see the power of compounding?

Think about this for a second. How much of that money is principal and how much is interest? Let's do the math. Using the example of twenty years, you have put in $9,700 of your own money ($100 initial deposit plus $40/month x 240 months). If you have $24,189 that would mean $14,489 is pure interest.

What about the forty-year example? Your own deposits would total $19,300 ($100 initial deposit plus $40/month x 480 months). Yet, you would have

$136,467, which means that $117,167 is pure interest. Can you say "free money"?

Let's step it up a bit

Imagine if you could put more than $40 a month away. Let's say you've managed to cut some expenses out and were able to up that monthly savings number to $100. Assuming the same scenario, starting with a $100 deposit, 8% interest compounded annually you would see this:

After 5 years	$7,750
After 10 years	$18,990
After 20 years	$59,773
After 40 years	$337,909

Can you say "comfortable retirement"? I realize that retirement is probably the last thing on your mind at this age, but it shouldn't be. What if you could retire early? Does retiring at forty-five *interest* you? (Funny how that word *interest* can be used in different ways.)

Here's the most important point I want you to take from this section. Start early! The more time you have, the more interest will be compounded. If you are able to save even more per month or earn more than 8%, as in the previous examples, you could hit the million dollar mark—if you start early enough.

There are tons of great websites that will allow you to play with different financial calculators. Check these sites out to start:

www.moneychimp.com: Click the calculators link.

www.bankrate.com: Click the calculators link. Tons of different scenarios!

Let's talk about your dreams and goals

It is so important to have dreams and goals for your-self. It fuels the soul with inspiration and determination. Having something that touches your heart and mind, whatever it is, will stir up feelings of hope, excitement and passion. We, as human beings, need that.

So, what does that have to do with savings? Well, most dreams and goals have something to do with money, in one way or another. It might be to make a certain income per year, it might be to give a certain amount every year to charity, or it may be to start a business venture that you've always wanted. It may even be a year-long trip around the world! Whatever those dreams, having good spending and savings habits will be an integral part of whether you reach those goals or not.

Learning how to save early, having the discipline necessary to consistently save and understanding the importance of savings early will prove to be a necessary foundation for your success. It takes planning ahead, delayed gratification, and just plain old smart sense.

At the time of this writing, the country is in an economic crisis. As I mentioned in an earlier chapter, people are losing their homes at record levels, jobs are being lost by the thousands, and people are afraid, anxious, and panicking. It is a challenging time for many. But, those who have a savings account in place are able to weather this storm better than others. As the stock market has taken a serious hit, those savings accounts have been hit as well. We have all been affected. But, if you diversify your funds as mentioned in the financial markets chapter, you should come out okay.

In these unusual times, even the best investor is affected. I'm not suggesting you will dodge the markets, nobody can. What I am saying is this: the better prepared you are and the wiser you are with your money, the better you will come out of this type of situation. Having said all that, this type of recession and housing market is not a regular occurrence. But, being prepared is wise, any way you look at it.

Bottom line is this: be diligent about your savings, take it seriously, plan ahead and keep that vision of financial independence in the forefront of your thoughts—not the newest gadget or stereo system for your car.

How should you allocate your savings?

The allocation of your savings will depend upon your age. As you get older and have more financial obligations, more of your money will go towards your needs, such as car, rent, and life.

Let's break it up into two different age groups. Ages 12–16 will have one set of allocation rules, and 16 and older will have another.

So, let's talk about 12–16 year olds. Since you don't have the responsibilities of a car and other expenses just yet, you are able to allocate more towards savings (for your car). You also don't have other need requirements. Here is my recommendation for the allocation of your income. By the way, this income includes money from a job, money from gifts, such as birthday money, jobs around the house, babysitting or any other source of income.

If you are 12–16 years old you should allocate:

30%	Play money
30%	Short-term savings
30%	Long-term savings
10%	Giving back

Play money: Thirty percent of your income can go towards just having plain old fun. This may be eating out with friends, buying a new gadget, going to the movies, or downloading your favorite music, etc. Whatever your little heart desires. If you have a cell phone and you have a monthly bill to pay, you can take it out of play money or short-term savings. It just depends on what you are saving for and how important that item is. Either way, you need to budget for that obligation.

Short term savings: Thirty percent should go to short-term savings. This category would include things like a new laptop you may want, a new cell phone, maybe a new technology item, etc. Try to keep this category for things that will benefit you somehow. For example, the new laptop can help with school projects, while the new cell phone will help you text faster. Yippee. (I'm being a bit sarcastic here, so think twice before you buy the cell phone.)

Long term savings: Thirty percent of your money should go to long-term savings. This would include money for your car, starting your investment account, or even college. Having money as a cushion for unforeseen circumstances is a good mindset to get into early. This is money you should not touch!

Giving back: Ten percent should go back to the world somehow. I recommend you find a charity that touches your heart somehow and make regular contributions. You can also give back to your religious organization or a local family in need. Giving back is so important, as I discuss in another chapter.

If you are 16 years or older, you should allocate:

50%	Needs
30%	Wants (short-term savings)
10%	Long-term savings
10%	Giving back

Needs: This would include all your expenses relating to your car, including car payments, car insurance, car maintenance and gas. It would also include cell phone payments, rent, utilities, food, and other needs. These expenses will obviously be much different when you move out of your parents' home. Either way, 50% should go towards needs. As you become an adult and have additional obligations, your allocations should follow closely to this model.

Wants: This would include two different umbrellas. One umbrella would be play money, such as entertainment, DVDs, eating out, etc. The other umbrella would be short-term savings for those same items I mentioned above. The wants category covers both play and short-term savings because you now have more financial obligations.

Long term savings: Personally, I would like to see more than 10% of your money go to long-term savings. If you can bring your expenses down (needs), try to add to long-term savings. This money will ramp up your investment accounts, perhaps set you up for buying your first piece of real estate or starting your own business. This becomes a question of your priorities. As mentioned earlier, the sooner you start saving, the sooner the compounding can start. We all like free money.

Giving back: The same 10% rule applies that I mentioned earlier. It's a wonderful feeling to help others.

So, overall, I hope you realize the importance of savings. It comes down to lifestyle choices and healthy habits. Just like I mentioned earlier, it's just like eating healthy. Good choices will bring good results. It's not always easy, I'll give you that. And, just like dieting, it's okay to cheat once in a while. But, you need to have an overall healthy perspective on your finances, with a solid foundation in place. I've seen so many situations where a person's savings account has rescued them through a tough time. Unfortunately, these challenging times can come at us fast, so you won't have time to prepare. Whether it is unforeseen medical expenses, a surprise job loss or other personal financial hits, it always helps to be prepared.

Wealth Building Tool #6

Investing Basics to Know Now

It's very exciting to think about starting to invest. Investing is all about making the money you have, making you *more* money. There are many options to consider and some basics to know before taking that leap. As with everything I've discussed in this book, it's important to do your homework and have a good understanding of what you are doing before you jump in. You'll be learning many new concepts and a new vocabulary that may seem overwhelming at first. Don't let this stop you. Doing nothing will cost you money in the long run. Enjoy the learning process and don't do anything until you fully understand what you are doing.

I mentioned earlier that investing is about making the money you have make you more money. The two most popular ways to do this is investing in real estate and investing in the stock market. (As a side note, *investing in yourself* is on the top of this list, but not the topic of this chapter.) This chapter is going to cover the stock market basics. Many people have made fortunes in both the real estate market and the stock market. My suggestion is that you tap into both, but only when you are ready.

Here's a quick overview of the topics I'm going to cover:

- Definitions of some of the vocabulary you will hear
- Type of stocks
- Type of bonds
- Mutual funds—a great consideration for you
- Cash equivalents that offer less risk
- What diversification means and why you must have it

Let me start by saying this information will be basic in nature. I want to introduce this world to you, without "fire hosing" you. There are many wonderful books that will teach you advanced techniques, such as trading options, understanding commodities, charting, and so much more. The information in this book will be a great foundation for you to get started.

If this information seems a bit hard to follow, just reread it and take in what you can. Referring back to this information is a great way to take this in, little by little.

Some definitions

I realize the basic definitions can be boring, but it helps to understand some of the vocabulary as you gain momentum here. Try to stay with it. If necessary, come back and refer to it later.

As you watch the market, you will gain a better understanding of what these words mean. For starters, I will give you the simple definitions.

Bear Market: A time where there is widespread pessimism in the financial markets and there has been a long period of stock prices falling. Simply put, market's going down.

Bull Market: A prolonged period of time where stock prices rise faster than the historical average. (People are happy because their stock values are going up.)

Diversification: Allocating your funds into various investment types to reduce your overall risk. Some investments will do better than others at any given time. You must diversify.

Dow (or DJIA): The Dow Jones Industrial Average. It the *price weighted average* of thirty significant stocks traded on the New York Stock Exchange and the NASDAQ. The Dow was invented by Charles Dow in 1896 and originally tracked only twelve stocks The list grew to its current size of thirty stocks in 1928. It is the single most watched index in the world and includes companies like General Electric, Disney, Exxon, and Microsoft. When you hear TV networks discussing "the market being up or down," they are generally referring to the Dow.

NYSE: The New York Stock Exchange is the oldest and largest stock exchange in the United States. It still uses a large trading floor where brokers of buyers and sellers do their transactions.

NASDAQ: The National Association of Securities Dealers Automated Quotation System. This is a computerized system that facilitates the trading of stocks. Unlike the NYSE, the NASDAQ does not have a physical trading place that brings actual buyers and sellers together. It was created in 1971 and provides price quotations for over 5,000 actively traded stocks. The NASDAQ is traditionally home to many high tech stocks, such as Intel, Dell, and Cisco.

S&P 500: The Standard and Poor's index of 500 stocks chosen for market size, liquidity and industry grouping, among other factors. The S&P 500 is one of the most commonly used benchmarks for the overall U.S. stock market. The Dow was at one time the most renowned index for U.S. stocks, but because it contains only thirty companies, most people agree that the S&P 500 is a better representation of the U.S. market. In fact, many consider it to be *the* definition of the market.

Earnings per share: The total earnings of a company divided by their number of shares outstanding.

Inflation: The term used to represent a rise in prices. Inflation usually occurs when there is too much money in circulation and not enough goods and services. Prices will rise when there is this excess demand.

Recession: A significant decline in activity across the economy, typically lasting 6–18 months. The technical indicator of a recession is two consecutive quarters of negative economic growth as measured by a country's gross domestic product (GDP). Recession is a normal, although unpleasant, part of the business cycle.

Money market fund: This is a mutual fund that invests in short-term, low-risk securities. The money is very liquid (which means you can get it any time) and comes with a lower risk, which means lower return. It usually offers a better rate than your bank checking and saving accounts though.

Mutual fund: An investment vehicle that is made up of a pool of funds collected from many investors for the purpose of investing in securities such as stocks, bonds, money market instruments, and similar assets. Mutual funds are operated by money managers, who invest the fund's capital and attempt to produce capital gains and income for the fund's investors. One of the main advantages of mutual funds is that they give small investors access to professionally managed, diversified portfolios of equities, bonds, and other securities, which would be quite difficult (if not impossible) to create with a small amount of capital. This is a great way for you to start investing in the stock market.

Stock: A holder of stock (a shareholder) has a claim to a part of the corporation's assets and earnings. In other words, a shareholder is an owner of a company. Ownership is determined by the number of shares a person owns relative to the number of outstanding shares. For example, if a company has 1,000 shares of stock outstanding and one person owns 100 shares, that person would own and have claim to 10% of the company's assets. There are two main types of stock: common and preferred. Common stock usually entitles the owner to vote at shareholders' meetings and to receive dividends. Preferred stock generally does not have voting rights, but has a higher claim on assets and earnings than the common shares. For example, owners of preferred stock receive dividends before common shareholders and have priority in the event that a company goes bankrupt and is liquidated.

There are many more definitions that pertain to the financial markets, but these are some key ones with which to start. As mentioned earlier, you will find a full glossary at the end of the book. There is also a great website for more advanced definitions and market information: www.investopedia.com.

So, let's talk stocks

As mentioned in the definition section, a stock is basically part ownership of a company. Pretty cool stuff! If the company does well and has good earnings and growth, the stock value (price) will generally go up. If the opposite happens and the company does poorly, the value goes down. The trick, of course, is to know which one of the thousands of stocks to purchase.

Over the long term, stocks have historically outperformed all other investments. From 1926 to 2006, the S&P 500 returned an average annual 10.4% gain.

On the flip side, do not invest in stocks if you need the money in the short term. Over the short term, stocks fluctuate based on everything from interest rates to gas prices to the latest hurricane. If you need the money to purchase something in less than 3–5 years, I do not recommend buying stock. It would be a total bummer if it was time to buy a car or your first home, only to find your money worth less than when you started. For this type of time frame, I recommend treasuries (more on that later) or money market accounts.

When it comes time to invest in the stock market, I'm going to recommend you start with a mutual fund. A mutual fund allows you to diversify into different sectors (businesses that have different products and services). In other words, you will spread out your risk if you have your money in different companies, within different arenas. I'll cover more on mutual funds shortly, but for now, just know that when you get started, consider mutual funds over a single company stock.

So, how do you decide which stock? This is where your research and due diligence comes in. By the way, don't buy a stock on a recommendation from a friend. Although friends always mean well, make sure to research the stock yourself and purchase on the fundamental and/or technical analysis.

This can be a bit advanced, so take it slow and refer back to it often. For fun, you can watch a company that offers a product you enjoy. If you love Nike shoes, watch Nike. If you love Coke, watch Coca Cola. You get the idea. You absolutely must "paper trade" stocks before you put your real money in the trade. Paper trading means that you "buy" a stock with pretend money. I'll call it your monopoly money. You don't actually buy the stock with real funds, you just pretend you bought at a certain price and time, based on your homework, and then sold it when you thought it was a good time. You then track your profit or losses. This is a great way to get your feet wet and gain confidence at the same time. There are several websites that allow you to set up an account for free to paper trade.

So, how do you analyze a stock? There are two popular ways that companies are analyzed.

Fundamental analysis means analyzing a stock based on earnings, revenues, future growth, return on equity, profit margins, and other data to determine a company's underlying value and potential for future growth. With fundamental analysis you are trying to determine a company's intrinsic value as well. (Intrinsic value is the value given to a company based on underlying *perception of value*. McDonald's would be an example of a company with intrinsic value.) You basically are looking at their books to determine if this company is strong, with a favorable future.

Technical analysis does not try to determine intrinsic value; rather the analysis is focused on market activity, such as past prices and volume. Technical analysts use charts and other tools to identify patterns that may suggest future activity. Even though charts are imperative, it's interesting to note, the biggest single determiner of stock prices is earnings.

Although this piece of information is a bit advanced, I wanted you to be aware that these categories exist. Stocks can be broken down into four different categories: large cap, mid-cap, small cap and international. "Cap" is short for capitalization, which is the total stock market value of all the shares of a company's stock. This is calculated by multiplying the stock price by the number of shares outstanding.

Generally speaking, large cap stock refers to companies with a market capitalization of greater than $5 billion, while small cap refers to companies with a market capitalization of less than $3 billion. Mid-cap are those that fall between the two. International is a non-U.S. company.

On to the bonds

Bonds are like an IOU. You get to lend a borrower some money, and they in return promise to pay you back that money, plus interest. A specific date (maturity date) and interest rate (the coupon rate) are in place as well. The main categories of bonds are corporate bonds, municipal bonds, and governmental bonds.

U.S. treasury bonds (governmental) are referred to as notes, bills, or bonds, depending upon their maturity duration. If you hear the term "treasuries," it's referring to the governmental bonds, notes, and bills.

A treasury bill (also called T-bill) has a maturity of less than one year, a treasury note has a maturity between one and ten years, and a bond has a maturity greater than ten years.

Here's an example: If you were to buy a $1,000 bond, with a coupon rate of 4% simple interest, payable in two years, you would get $20 interest paid semi-annually, or $40 per year. That means you would get paid twice per year. At the end of the two years, you would receive your $1,000 principal back.

With a treasury bill (maturity less than one year), you won't receive interest semi-annually. You would actually buy the bill at a *discount* and receive the face value of the bill at maturity. The discounted amount would depend on the interest rate and duration to maturity.

Governmental bonds are considered very safe, but understand there are no guarantees with bonds. There is risk, which is why it's important to do your homework. Many bonds are rated by agencies, such as Moody's and Standard and Poor's. These agencies grade the financial standing of the issuer to help you make better decisions.

Like most investments in the financial markets, there is a risk vs. reward payoff. The higher risk issuer (generally graded lower) will offer higher returns (higher interest rates). You will need to decide your risk tolerance and length of time you have to invest to determine which bond makes sense.

Again, when you are starting out, I would recommend you look into mutual funds. These are a great way to stay diversified, while investing in bonds of different types.

One more thing about bonds: depending upon the type of bond in which you invest, there can be some tax benefits involved. It is beyond the scope of this book to discuss the tax advantages, but just know that when you decide to invest in bonds, be sure to explore the tax consequences.

Mutual funds

As I've mentioned earlier, mutual funds are a great way to get started in the financial markets. They are very simple to invest in, very efficient, easily liquidated (meaning you can get your money out quickly), and allow for easy diversification. There are many different types of funds from which to choose, and asking yourself three basic questions will help you decide which makes the most sense for you.

First, ask yourself, "What is my goal?" Are you looking for more income or safety?

Second, "What is my time frame?" Will you need this money in the next few months or is this investment for longer term needs? As mentioned earlier, I wouldn't recommend the stock market if you need the money in three years or less. You are better off putting those funds into a money market account (there are money market mutual funds, too) and protecting your principal.

Third, "How much risk am I willing to take?" Remember, the riskier the investment, the higher return you will normally receive. If you aren't comfortable with the riskier investments, understand your return may not be as good. This is a very personal decision, and either way is completely acceptable.

If you have a longer time horizon, such as five years or more, you can afford to go with a bit more riskier mutual fund. You must have the stomach to ride the ups and downs of the market, but over the long run, stocks generally do well.

So, what are your choices?

Here's the list of varies types of mutual funds.

Money Market Funds: These funds generally invest in short term U.S. treasury bills, certificate of deposits (CDs) or commercial paper. Although they are not FDIC insured, they are considered very safe investments. These will tend to have better returns than savings accounts, but because they are considered lower risk investments, the returns won't be anything exciting. Sometimes boring is good, especially if you will need the money in the near future.

Bond Funds: These funds are a pool of bonds, typically invested in corporate, municipal or government bonds. Just like the bonds described earlier, they are typically more conservative than a stock. Bond funds fall between the money market fund and stock funds when discussing risk and reward. They are less risky than stock funds, but more risky than money market funds. As a result, you will typically receive a higher return in a bond fund than you would a money market fund, but less than a stock fund.

Stock funds: There is a huge choice of stock funds, with various risk levels associated with them. Some funds' primary goal is income, while others are more growth focused. Deciding which one makes the most sense for you will depend on how you answered those previous three questions. It's important to understand that as the market goes up or down, the value of your investment will go up and down. There is no guarantee that you won't lose money. In fact, you will see your account fluctuate day to day, but remember, when you invest in the stock market, you should be investing for the long term. By long term, I mean at least four to five years.

Hybrid funds: This type of fund invests in both stocks and bonds. They are also called balanced funds, blended funds, or asset allocation funds. These funds have the goal of both investment growth and stability. I personally like this type of fund, as it diversifies for me.

Some final thoughts on mutual funds

When shopping for a mutual fund, make sure you do your homework. I know, I know, you've heard that before. Research the past performance, and watch for fees. Although past performance will never guarantee any future results, it's always good to compare to other funds. I recommend a no-load (which means no commissions) fund. You can research all this information very easily online.

Cash equivalents

Examples of these investments include checking accounts, savings accounts, money market accounts, CDs, and T-bills. CDs (certificate of deposits) can be shorter term, such as three months, or longer term, sometimes five years. This investment type falls into the category of lower risk, lower return. But, if you need your money in the short term or for emergency money, this is a great place to stash the cash.

Diversify, diversify, diversify

After reading through the various types of investment options, I hope you see the importance of being diversified. The market can be very volatile and putting all your eggs in one basket can be a costly mistake. Having your funds in various growth, income, bond and money market accounts is important. Typically when one aspect of the market is doing well, the other is not, and vice versa.

Once you decide which fund(s) you like, consider what is called "dollar cost averaging." Let me explain. Rather than investing all your money at one time into a fund, consider buying into that fund in increments. This will *average out* the cost of that investment.

For example, if you had $2,000 to invest, consider buying into the fund in $500 increments over four consecutive months. This allows for buying more shares when the price is lower. This also lessens the risk of investing a larger amount at the wrong time. Plus, an added benefit is you will get into the habit of investing on a regular, monthly basis. This will be huge over time.

I haven't even touched on the other markets, namely commodities, oil and gas, precious metals, real estate investment trusts, or international funds. This information is much more advanced and not necessary to get yourself started in the markets. Take it slow, do what makes you comfortable and confident, and continue to learn!

I've given you enough information to get your feet wet and start exploring. Have fun with it, but take it seriously. This is your hard-earned money we are talking about!

you a general idea of

CREDIT HISTORY

be judged on its own
of information

Wealth Building Tool #7

The Nuts and Bolts of Your Credit Score

You've heard about it on commercials. You probably hear people talking about it. The "it" is credit scores. So, what is a credit score? Why is it so important? How do you find out what your score is?

This is one of those topics where I may get the "deer in the headlights" look. Well, snap out of it. This is one of the most important subjects and one that can cost you or save you a ton of money and heartache.

Your credit score is, in simple terms, very similar to your grades in school. You are *graded* based on your performance and abilities. In this case, your performance is related to your ability to manage credit. Credit can come in the form of a credit card, a car loan, a mortgage, or a personal loan.

Credit scores range from 300–850. So, what's a good score? Well, it depends on who you ask. Most would agree that an excellent score is 740 or above. Consider this an A in school. Anything below 620 is considered poor, or risky. A score of 700–740 is generally considered good, while 680–700 is fair. So, if I were the teacher (as Mom, I am), I would give you the following grades:

A	740+
B	700–740
C	680–700
D	620–680
F	620 or below

When you get your own credit card, it is your sole responsibility to pay that bill on time and preferably pay it in full, every single month. (If you know you can't pay the bill in full, you shouldn't make that purchase. A few exceptions are allowed, such as an emergency, that's just Mom's rule. More details to follow.) Making those payments on time, and in full, is like turning in A work at school.

So who gives these scores to you anyway?

The most widely used credit scores are FICO scores, which were created by Fair Isaac Corporation. Lenders buy the scores from three major credit reporting agencies. The three major credit reporting agencies in the U.S. are Experian, Equifax, and TransUnion. These agencies maintain your credit records and other information about you. The records are called your credit report, and this report is what lenders look at before they decide to give you credit. Your credit score will also determine the interest rate and other terms of your loan. Bad credit equals bad interest rate; good credit equals good interest rate. Needless to say, you will save big money over time if you have a lower interest rate. This is why you must keep your credit scores high and take responsibility when using credit. It will cost you dearly if you don't.

What you can expect to find on your credit report

Just like a report card will give you more than just your grades, your credit report gives more than just your credit score. There is all types of information about you on your report. Here are the main sections:
- ID section
- Credit history section
- Collection accounts section
- Public records
- Additional information
- Inquiry section

ID section

In this section, you will find simple, basic information. Your name, address, social security number, date of birth and spouse's name (when that someday occurs).

Credit history section

This section is basically the meat and potatoes of your report. It lists all your open and paid credit accounts. This section will give details such as company name, account number, whose account it is (if had joint or cosigner), date the credit was opened, the history on months reported, last activity information, terms, outstanding balance, high credit, past due and status. It will also list any late payment information.

Collection accounts section

This section is where you will find any accounts that went to collection. (I know this will never apply to you.) It's a good idea to keep your eyes on this section, as there might be something here that isn't yours. Errors on credit reporting do occur, so keep tabs.

Public records

Here you will find a listing of public record items that are either, local, state or federal court related. A few examples include bankruptcy, tax liens, judgments, or collection accounts.

Additional information

This section discloses past addresses and previous employers.

Inquiry section

If any business has pulled your credit in the past twenty-four months, their name will appear here. Too many inquiries can harm your credit score, so don't give your authorization to pull credit unless it is absolutely necessary.

What factors go into your score?

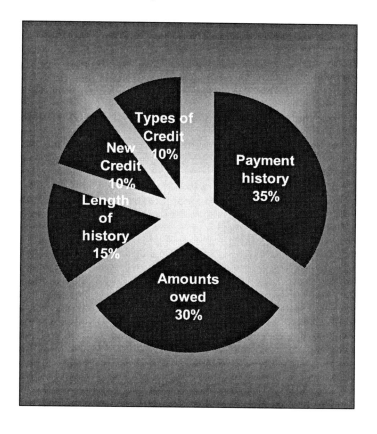

Let's break this down, while keeping it simple. I'll give you the basic, important information you need to know. Credit scoring is complicated and the calculations remain a mystery. Like Coca-Cola, nobody can give you the exact recipe, but we can get enough information to get the job done. In this case, get your credit scores up and keep them up. I just can't tell you how it's calculated.

Payment history accounts for 35% of your credit score. This basically tells us whether you have made your payments on time. As you can see, this weighs heavy on the score, as it accounts for 35%. Lenders want to know how responsible you are with managing money and your payments. Making *one* late payment is not an automatic score killer, but it will drop your score, so it's important to keep your bills organized and make sure nothing is overlooked. These payments can be on credit cards, car loans, any finance company or mortgage loans. I suggest you keep all your bills in one location and pay them twice per month, usually the first and fifteenth of the month. But, watch the credit card due dates, as they will differ from card to card. If you wish, call the credit card companies and try to schedule the billing dates to be the same.

Amounts owed accounts for 30% of your credit score. Simply put, this looks at what you owe on credit as a percentage of the total credit available to you. To keep your scores up, maintain that percentage below 35%. For example, let's say you have a credit card with available credit of $1,000. If you use that card and your balance goes above approximately $350, your scores will be affected. In this example, keep the balance below $350. The credit bureaus don't like to see you "maxed out," as it implies you may not make your payment on time, if at all. Given this information, you may be tempted to run out and get a bunch of credit cards so you have a lot of *available* credit, but be careful. Too many cards can lower your score, as it increases risk. What's the magic number of cards? It depends. Start out with one or two major credit cards (AMEX, VISA, Discover or MasterCard). You can add a gas card or department store card, but don't add more than one or two. Having five or so credit lines is fine, especially as a young adult. If you have a car loan, that would count as a credit line as well. More is not necessarily better with credit cards.

Length of credit history accounts for 15% of your credit score. Basically, the longer you have a credit history the better. This is why you don't want to close older credit cards, even if you don't use them. Cut them up and stop using them, just don't close the account. On the flip side, don't fret if you are new to credit and don't have much of a history. You can have high scores without history if the rest of your credit report looks good.

New credit accounts for 10% of your credit score. Too much of a good thing is a bad thing. Basically, you shouldn't go out and open a bunch of new accounts at once. It signals that you may be overextending yourself, or worse, are already in trouble. Also, newer accounts will lower your *average* account age, which will have a large impact if you don't have other credit information. This ties in with the previous section of length of credit history.

Types of credit accounts for 10% of your credit score. Simply stated, mix it up. Your score will improve if you have a healthy mix of credit. For example: credit cards, retail accounts, installment loans (car payment), and mortgage loans. Remember, more is not necessarily better.

So, why the big deal?

As I mentioned early on, the credit score calculations are complicated and much goes into them. I have discussed the primary, most important aspects of your score. But why are they so important? What's the best way to get good scores?

For starters, your credit scores are looked at by many people, not just lenders or car financing salesman.

Some employers will look at your credit scores to determine how responsible you are. Doesn't it make sense that if you are responsible with managing your money, you would be responsible as an employee? I think it makes total sense. Some insurance companies will also look at scores to determine pricing on your policies. Talk about a costly mistake if you let your scores drop. If you decide to rent an apartment or home before buying, landlords will pull credit to determine if they want to rent to you or not. It can be a risky proposition for them if your scores are poor. On the flip side, if you have excellent scores and are competing with another person for that rental, you may win out.

When it comes time to buy your first car, finance a big purchase, or buy your first home, your credit score will dictate the interest rate you pay. It will cost you dearly if you have poor credit. In some cases, you won't be able to get credit at all if the scores are too low. I can't stress enough how important it is to be on your game with your credit.

As a note, I do not suggest you finance big purchases. When it comes time to buy furniture, a laptop, or similar big ticket items, pay cash. If you can't pay cash, wait until you can. Feel free to put it on a credit card only if you know you will pay it off in full when the bill arrives.

How to get a copy of your credit report

As of this writing, you are allowed to pull your own credit report once per year for free. If you pull it yourself, it will not count as an inquiry on your report, which is preferable. Go to www.annualcreditreport.com for the free report. This site does not give you your credit score, just the report. You can go to www.myfico.com to obtain your scores, but they charge a nominal fee. You can also order your credit report directly from the credit reporting agencies. Here is their contact info:

Equifax:	www.equifax.com	800-685-1111
Experian:	www.experian.com	888-397-3742
TransUnion:	www.transunion.com	800-888-4213

If you ever found an error on your report, you would need to contact the above agencies to dispute. If you report an error to the agency, they must investigate and respond to you within thirty days.

How to get credit scores up and keep them up

Here are a few suggestions for getting those scores up:

- Keep balances low on credit cards and other revolving credit. (Remember the amount owed I mentioned?)

- Don't close those cards that you don't use, especially if they are older cards. Cut them up and stop using them, just leave them open.
- Don't go out and open a bunch of new credit cards that you don't need just to increase available credit. That could backfire on you.
- Pay your bills on time, pay your bills on time, and always remember to *pay your bills on time.* I realize that was annoying, but I want that stuck in your brain.
- When it's time to buy your car or home, shop for the loan within a short period of time, preferably two to three weeks. Each inquiry won't be considered a single inquiry that way.
- When the nice person at the department store offers you 10% off your purchase if you open a credit card, smile and say, "No, thank you." Unless you need the credit, don't open just to open.
- Using credit cards to pay for gas or food, knowing full well you will pay that off in full, will help raise your score. Showing that you can *use and pay* on a regular, consistent basis will exhibit responsible behavior.
- If you have a credit limit on a card, never go over that limit. The credit card companies will

allow you to do that sometimes, but your scores will drop, as you will be maxed out.

- If any of this is confusing and overwhelming, don't fret. You are not alone. Just make sure you get educated before making any decisions and don't be pressured into anything.
- If all else fails, call someone experienced whom you trust.

I realize this was a lot of information to take in one sitting. Use this as a reference and reread it as necessary. Getting on top of your credit and staying on top of it will benefit you more than you realize. You truly won't appreciate this until you have experienced life a little.

Wealth Building Tool #8

It's Time—Your First Home

Note for parents: This information is geared toward the older child. Younger kids will benefit from this, but the older (20+) child will better relate, as they may be thinking about buying a home in the near future. The following information is a bit more technical and advanced; however, it is a wonderful reference tool for later. I would recommend reading this now, but referring back to this when actually buying a home as well.

Although you may not be looking at buying a home anytime soon, this is invaluable information to know early on. Some of this information can be a bit overwhelming, but if you read it slowly and fully understand it, you will reap priceless rewards. I do admit, it can be a bit dry at times, but please stick with me on this. Reread it as often as needed and use as a reference tool for later.

Let me start by saying, I'm not sure who's more excited—me or you. Buying your first new home is one of the most exciting things you will experience. Having independence and a place to call your own will bring you such a feeling of freedom and strength.

First, let me say, how very proud I am of you. I can't wait to see how you decorate, the colors you choose, and the style of furniture and…oh… sorry, I digress. Can't help it, that's what moms do. Seriously though, it's going to be a blast watching you put *your home* together. Just keep it cleaner than you've kept your room.

So, where do you start when it's time to buy your first place? There are many different elements that go into buying a home, but when broken down into separate subjects, they become easy to handle. Here are the key elements that we'll discuss:

1) Credit scores
2) Down payment
3) Closing costs
4) Loan types
5) Where to buy

Credit scores

I covered credit scores at great length in another chapter, but let me emphasize how important a good credit score is to your mortgage payment. Without a good score (at the time of this writing, a good score would be 720 or above), your interest rate will be higher, costing you thousands of dollars over time. The lenders (banks who would lend you money) are going to charge you a higher interest rate if they feel you are a higher risk borrower. The credit score tells them how well you've been able to manage your credit, which in turn, gives them an indication of how much risk you are to them. Higher risk equals higher rate. Lower risk equals lower rate. That goes for everything you purchase on credit.

Let's use an example that may be easier to understand. These numbers are for instructional purposes only and do not represent today's rates. Let's say you buy a home and your mortgage is $250,000. A thirty-year fixed, fully amortized mortgage (fully amortized simply means you are paying principal and interest in your monthly mortgage payment) with a 720 score may have an interest rate of 6.50%. Your mortgage payment only (not including taxes and insurance) would be $1,580.17. Now, let's say your credit score is less than perfect, so the lender charges you 7.25%. Seems like no big deal, but check out this math. Now your payment goes to $1,705.44, a difference of $125.27 per month. That's $1,503.25 a year. That's almost enough to pay an entire month's mortgage payment. If you stay in the house for five years, or don't refinance out of that loan, that costs you $7,516.24 for that five-year period—even more if you stay in longer. I can't emphasize enough how imperative it is to get your credit scores up and keep them up.

At the time of this writing, our banking system is going through an incredible crisis as a result of loans that were made that shouldn't have been. Homes are being foreclosed upon at record levels (that's when the homeowner stops making the mortgage payment and the bank has to take the home back, resulting in the homeowner losing their house). Banks would lend to borrowers with poor credit, commonly called sub-prime loans, and in some cases offered 100% financing. That means the borrower didn't have to give any of their own money (down payment) when they originally bought the house.

As a result of this, lenders and large brokerage houses are closing their doors due to huge losses. The lenders that are left standing are considerably more conservative with their approval guidelines, meaning they are stricter when reviewing your loan application. Time will only tell what will happen with the lenders, how tight their underwriting guidelines will become and how this financial crisis will play out. But, one thing is for sure: your credit has to be excellent if you ever hope to buy a home and pay an attractive rate. Another good example of why you need to watch your credit cards and spending habits.

Down payment

The down payment represents the amount of money you bring to the table. It's your hard-earned, cold cash that you deposit when you buy your home. It is also referred to as your "'equity." Let me digress here one minute regarding your equity. As real estate values go up and down, your equity value will increase or decrease. The beautiful thing about real estate is that over time, typically values will increase and you will enjoy an increased equity position, even though you didn't put more money down. That's why real estate is a wonderful addition to a balanced, diversified investment portfolio. As I've mentioned earlier, the present housing crisis is creating a downward pressure on prices, increased inventory, and increased foreclosures. In my book, this is a wonderful buying opportunity. Again, real estate is part of your diversification plan.

Okay, back to the fun. To get the most attractive rate on your loan, you will need at least a 20% down payment. For example, if you buy a home for $300,000, a 20% down payment would equal $60,000, resulting in a loan amount of $240,000. If you're thinking, "Where am I going to get *that* kind of money?" don't despair. (I told you to stop spending money on those silly video games—sorry, had to put my plug in.)

There are loans available that require less than 20% down, that are have competitive rates, assuming, yes, you have good credit. FHA is a great alternative requiring only 3½% down payment (as of this writing) and allows for gift funds, seller-paid closing costs, and less than perfect credit scores. FHA stands for Federal Housing Administration, which is a governmental agency that insures mortgages. "Seller paid closing costs" means that the seller of the home is allowed to pay for some of *your* closing costs, such as title, escrow, appraisal, and more. We'll touch more on that in a bit. Basically, it helps you get into the home with less of your cash out of pocket. There is a price to pay for this luxury, but it's not too bad.

Anytime you put less than 20% down on a home, you are required to pay PMI, which stands for *private mortgage insurance*. In simple terms, it's an insurance policy to protect lenders in case a borrower defaults (stops making his mortgage payments). You have to pay the insurance premium, which adds to your monthly payment. With FHA loans you have this monthly insurance premium, plus an up-front insurance cost. This is what I was referring to when I said there is a price to pay for the luxury of an FHA loan.

FHA is not the only alternative for less than 20% down. There are other programs, but you will always have PMI to pay. Prior to the subprime meltdown that we are experiencing today, lenders were allowed to do

100% financing. Typically, the borrower would have an 80% first loan and a 20% second loan, eliminating the PMI issue. (As long as the first loan is 80% or less, there was no PMI.) Borrowers were not required to put any down payment, which meant zero equity at time of purchase.

When home values declined, borrowers found themselves in upside-down positions, which meant they owed more money than what the house was worth. Combine that with the interest rate adjusting if they didn't have a fixed-rate loan and high unemployment, and you have the disaster we are experiencing today. Many loans were given to people who couldn't afford to buy the home in the first place. As a result, we are experiencing families losing their homes at record levels.

So, why all this information? I never want to see you experience this pain and loss. You need to make sure you are ready to afford the payment, have a down payment, get the proper loan, and don't buy more home than you should. And always keep your credit score up. I know I sound like a broken record, but I can't emphasize that enough.

So, back to the down payment. There is no secret science to having a nice down payment—spend less and save more. If you start saving early and invest it wisely, you will have a nice down payment before you know it. Watch the spending habits, as discussed earlier, and you'll be in your own home sooner than you think.

Closing costs

Closing costs are those costs that you have to pay when you buy or refinance a home. There are many people and fingers involved, and everybody gets paid, one way or another. Closing costs can be broken down into two different categories: non-recurring and recurring. You will also have a possible third category: impounds.

Let's start with **non-recurring**. Just as the name implies these are costs that *do not reoccur* each month. They are one-time costs associated with the purchase or refinance. Examples of these costs are title insurance, escrow (what we use in California, some states use attorneys), appraisal, underwriting (the person who works for the lender and reviews your loan—they give you the thumbs up or thumbs down), processing, recording fees, notary fees, and other small miscellaneous costs.

In addition, you will have the option to pay a *loan origination* or *loan discount fee.* This is also referred to as paying *points.* By paying a loan origination or discount fee (point), you are buying your interest rate down on your mortgage. If you decide to pay zero points, you will pay a slightly higher interest rate. One point equals one percent of your loan amount. Two points equals two percent of your loan amount. I would not recommend you ever pay more than one point. Always calculate the breakeven point to determine if it makes sense to pay the one point.

I know this can be a bit confusing so let's use an example:

Let's say your loan amount equals $200,000 (whether you buy or refinance, the same rules apply). If you decide to pay one point, that would cost you $2,000, which is *in addition* to your other nonrecurring closing costs. Let's say your rate would be 6.00% with one point, but if you chose zero points, your rate would be 6.25%. (This is typically, but not always the difference in rate, about 0.25%.) Your payment on a $200,000 mortgage at 6.00% would be $1,199.10 (fixed rate, principal and interest). Your payment at 6.25% would be $1,231.43, resulting in a difference of $32.33 per month. To determine if it makes sense to pay the point or not, we would divide the $2,000/32.33 to see how many months it would take before we broke even. In this example, it would take 61.86 months, or just over five years.

Basically what this means is that if we paid the $2,000 upfront, we wouldn't benefit from that expense until five years from now. In this case, I would not recommend you pay the point; it's too long before you get your money back. You will probably move or refinance that loan before that five-year term, so it doesn't make much sense. I like to see three years or less for a breakeven point before I recommend paying a point. Cash is king, especially when buying your first home, so paying that additional point may be tough. Having said all that, if the seller is willing to pay some closing costs, including a point, this can be a great way to buy your rate down.

Recurring costs are those that reoccur every month: interest payments, homeowners insurance, property taxes and where applicable, homeowners association dues. Depending upon what day of the month you close escrow, you will have prorated interest to pay. (I know this information can by dry and tough to follow, but hang with me here. This is important stuff.)

You will owe interest to the new lender for a portion of the month that you own the home. For example, if you close escrow on the tenth of the month, you will owe twenty days of interest to the lender (assuming a thirty-day month). This twenty days of interest is part of your closing costs that you need to pay at close of escrow.

Here's an interesting little side note. When you make your mortgage payment on the first of the month, you are actually paying for the *prior* month. For example, when you pay your mortgage on June 1, you are actually paying the interest for May. The technical term is "arrears." By the way, your payment is due on the first of the month, considered late on the fifteenth. Don't be late. Being late on a mortgage payment will hurt your credit score terribly. Some lenders won't even give you a loan if you have one thirty-day mortgage late.

Back to recurring costs. So, you will have the prorated interest we discussed. You will also have prorated property taxes, which essentially follows the same process as interest. Depending upon when you close escrow, you will owe property taxes from that date. Now, this gets a bit tricky.

Property taxes are paid twice per year. When we pay those taxes, we pay for six-month increments. Here in California, the first installment is due November 1 and is considered delinquent if not paid by December 10. The second installment is due February 1, delinquent April 10. It is beyond the scope of this book to explain how the property taxes work, but just know that you will owe a portion at the close of escrow. Make sure you do your homework and get an approximate amount due so you have a handle on your closing costs. Lenders are required to give you a good faith estimate at the beginning of your mortgage process, which will break these numbers down for you.

A one-year homeowner's insurance premium will also be due at time of closing. An exception would be if you purchase a condominium or townhome where the homeowners insurance is included with the home-owners association dues. Contact an insurance agent that you trust, or get referred to, to obtain a quote on a homeowners policy.

Impounds, also known as escrow accounts, are required when you put less than a 20% down payment. They are optional if you put 20% or more down. An impound account is an account that the lender has for you, like a saving account in your name, that accumulates your property taxes and homeowners insurance on a monthly basis. Every month you pay your normal mortgage payment, you would also include the monthly portion of taxes and insurance. This basically budgets that money for you. When those large expenses come due, the lender then pays that out of your impound account. Some people prefer it because if forces them to save for those expenses monthly. It doesn't require the discipline to save on their own. Others prefer to save themselves and enjoy the interest on the money they are saving. It really becomes a personal choice. If you are disciplined enough to save monthly, I would recommend you don't have the lender impound and you enjoy the interest on your own money while it sits in your savings account. I suggest having an automatic withdrawal set up with your checking account and a separate savings account for this expense. Having the money taken out automatically doesn't give you the choice to forget. Having said that, some lenders and states may require you to impound, so be sure to check beforehand.

I know this is a lot of information to take in. I also realize it can be a bit boring. Just refer back to it as needed. It's imperative you understand how this works. It can save you a lot of money and headache in the long run.

Loan types

This is an interesting topic, given the present credit crisis we are experiencing. Not too long ago, there were many more loan types available than there are today. Many of the creative loans that existed are partly to blame for this mess in the housing market today. This may, and probably will, change as time passes. Some loan types will be eliminated and some may be added. Time will tell.

Here are the main loan types today:

> Thirty-year fixed
> ARMs
> Pay option ARM
> Interest only

For the most part, sticking with the simple, vanilla type loan is best. By simple vanilla, I mean a thirty-year fixed, fully amortized loan. Basically this means that your rate is locked for thirty years, or the life of the loan, and pays down the principal and interest. There are no surprises with interest rate fluctuations, and you are paying off your mortgage over time. There are also fifteen- and twenty-year, fixed, fully amortized loans. The payments on these would be higher than the thirty-year because the loan is being amortized, or paid off, a lot quicker. Typically, though, the interest rates on these loans are lower than the thirty-year fixed. Be careful with the fifteen- or twenty-year loan, only because you are locked into that higher payment. If you ever have a financial issue arise, you must come up with the higher monthly payment when you may not be able to afford to. This is just something to think about when deciding which loan program to go with. With the fifteen or twenty-year loan, your equity is growing faster, which is certainly a nice benefit.

ARMs or adjustable rate mortgages are an alternative that may make sense for some. ARMs come in several forms: three year, five year, seven year and ten year are the most common. Basically, these loans offer fixed rates for the first 3/5/7/10 years, then the loan becomes adjustable, meaning the rate will fluctuate after that. I only recommend this type of loan if you know for certain that you will be out of this loan before the loan adjusts. This works well for those who plan to move or know they will be refinancing in the next few years. These loans typically have a lower interest rate, which is why people are attracted to them. If you end up staying with the loan for some reason, when your payment adjusts you may experience payment shock. This is how many people get in trouble. If you are considering this type of loan, be sure that you are out before the rate adjusts.

The **Pay Option ARM** is one that creates a lot of controversy. This type of loan has gotten a lot of people in trouble, if abused. If used properly, it can be advantageous. The problem is that most people don't use this loan properly. This loan gives you four payment options:

1) The minimum payment. Like a teaser payment, this does not fully pay your interest and principal. If you make this minimum payment only, your loan balance will increase over time.

2) Interest only payment. Pays the interest only portion of your payment. Your loan balance will not increase or decrease.

3) Fully amortized thirty-year (not fixed rate).

4) Fully amortized fifteen-year (not fixed rate and calculated to pay off loan in fifteen years).

As the name implies, it is an ARM, so the rate is not fixed.

Interest only loans are ones that payoff the interest-only portion. They are calculated in simple math terms: Principal x rate x time = interest.

$200,000 mortgage at 6.00% = $200,000 x 6.00% / 12 = $1,000 per month

Your loan balance will never decrease unless you make additional principal payments. These are beneficial to those who have a cash-flow issue, but know that they will be receiving a raise or promotion in the near future.

My side note: Some investors use these loans and take the portion that would normally pay down the principal and invest in the stock market or other investment vehicles. This is a great way to make your money work for you. Keep in mind, your equity earns you a zero rate of return. It's nice to have equity in your home, but it's not working for you. *You must be very disciplined and on your game to do this.* If done properly, you will actually have an accelerated loan payoff. The details of how this works is beyond the scope of this book. Again, do the homework and fully understand your options. Do not do this unless you fully understand the mechanics.

Having said all this about loan types, the safest, most conservative loan would be a thirty-year fixed, fully amortized loan. Most people prefer this loan type and for good reason. There aren't any surprises with rate adjustments, and you are paying off your loan over time.

Note: as of this writing in 2009, the pay option ARM loan has been eliminated. There are many changes being made rapidly due to the economic changes taking place. Adjustable rate mortgages and interest only mortgages may be eliminated in time as well. I left this information in the book, in the event these loan types return.

Where to buy

This should be a given—near your mom of course. Okay, you can stop the eye-rolling, please. In all seriousness, this is such a personal decision. Besides the obvious factors of family, friends and work, there are other important considerations.

In the real estate world you will hear, "location, location, location." For good reason. The specific location, even within the same city, can make a huge difference in your home's appreciation over time. Do your homework, talk to the local people, talk to several agents and take your time investigating. This will probably be the largest financial investment you make, so don't rush through it. You'll make some mistakes, as we all do, but that just makes for a better experience the second time.

From a purely investment perspective, find a location that has experienced strong real estate appreciation, has had strong growth in the work force, a climate that you enjoy, a low crime rate, and excellent school districts, just to name a few.

Sometimes just driving around a neighborhood, getting a sense of what people are doing to their homes, will give you an idea of the pride of ownership within the area. Take your time and enjoy the journey of searching.

Some states are more affordable than others, and it's best to find a home that feels right for you. I can tell you from personal experience that being near your family is a wonderful gift. The quality of your life is enhanced with your family and friends surrounding you.

Some final thoughts

It is beyond the scope of this book to go into the calculations that lenders use to approve you for a loan. Basically, they will look at your expenses relative to your income and use certain ratios to give you a yes or no vote. But beware, they may approve you for a loan that *may not feel comfortable for you*. If you are told that you can afford a $300,000 home, based on your ratios, but after doing the math, you are comfortable with the monthly payment on a $250,000 home, by all means follow your gut. Don't let someone talk you into a loan or home because it will earn them a bigger commission.

Also, make sure you have at least six months of living expenses tucked away in a savings account. This should include mortgage payment, property taxes, and homeowners insurance. Keep the money in a liquid account, such as a money market account, just in case you need it quickly. Ignore the temptation to tap into this money for furniture or other goodies for your new place. Put the money aside and forget you have it.

Having said all that, your new home will bring you so much joy as you make it your own. Sharing it with those around you will make for some serious fun. Don't forget to invite your mom over for dinner—I'll bring the dessert.

Wealth Building Tool #9

Give It Away: It's the Greatest Gift of All

"A generous man will prosper, he who refreshes others will himself be refreshed"
Proverbs 11:25

I have purposely left this chapter as the last one in the book. Not because it is the least important—no, quite the opposite. It is so important that I wanted this to be the last section you read, which will hopefully be on the forefront of your mind.

All this wealth knowledge, money skills and financial wisdom is not for accumulating things. It's not meant to teach you how to afford the fanciest car, biggest house, or latest gadget. This is not just about material wealth, but also about spiritual and emotional wealth.

Having a nice home and car is wonderful, but not at the expense of your financial freedom. By *my* definition, financial freedom is not only having the funds available to take care of you and your family, but also share it with the world and give back to society.

Side note for parents: Your kids are watching you! Nothing encourages your kids more than to see you do the same. Consider matching the donation dollar for dollar, which supports both the organization and your child. Work as a family to volunteer your time and decide where to allocate your family's contributions.

Don't get me wrong. I want you to enjoy the finer things in life. My desire is for you to live in a home that feels like your sanctuary away from the world, be able to afford dining out whenever you want, wear the clothes that please you, and simply enjoy life to its fullest. It is a delicate balancing act, as I don't want you focused on things. Those things will never bring you true happiness, at least not for long. Oftentimes, we spend money to fill an emotional void. Please try to avoid this and be aware of why you want something. Buying on a bad day or emotional whim will only create more stress for you when the bill arrives later. Enjoy your life and treat yourself to gifts that feed your soul, not the neighbors impression of you.

Giving away money isn't the only thing I want you giving away. I want you to share *you* with the world. Devote your time and skills to a cause that resonates with you. Take the time necessary to find your *purpose in life.* Why do you think God brought you here, at this time? That's a question that so many people struggle with, but when the answer is revealed, it can be life changing. You have so many gifts and talents to share, please embrace those and let them shine for everyone to see. Take your time and enjoy the journey to find that purpose. Be patient and know that it will be revealed at the right time. But you need to be looking for it. Seek it. Ask for it. Then be still.

I've always encouraged you to think in entrepreneurial terms. As I write this, there are some major shifts happening in our world, including our workforce. Gone are the days of stability and working for corporate America. Benefits, hours, and more are being taken away, bit by bit. As a result, many are looking at alternatives, namely being self-employed. Whether you work for someone else or take the entrepreneurial route, please be in a place of *purposeful service*. Find a way to make a difference in the world, find a way to give back, find a way to improve the lives of others. This will bring you more joy than the latest gadget, while feeding your soul with inner happiness.

In order to find the right path for yourself, I encourage you to take some quiet time and think about this: What are some of your *talents*? What are your shining *skills*? What do you *love* to do? How can you use this in a way that will generate cash for you *and* serve the world? Think about creating a business that utilizes your talents and skills that you also enjoy. Look for a business model or business plan that works for you.

You don't necessarily need to create a business model from scratch. Find one that works successfully, that is aligned with your value system. Allow your creativity to soar, and just think to yourself, "If I knew I couldn't fail, what would I want to do?"

There are no limits for you. You are an amazing person and can do anything you set your mind to. You just have to want it bad enough. You have to have a plan, define your dream, set your goals, and don't listen to any negative noise that you may hear. Surround yourself with positive people who believe in you and support you. Know that God put you here for a reason, for a purpose. Prosperity and abundance is his wish for you, but, again, not for the purpose of buying toys—big-boy or little-boy toys. Review the chapter on your mindset towards money and work to master that aspect. How you look at money, respect money, and understanding your beliefs toward money will be vital towards the management of your money.

I've always said that dying with millions in the bank is a tragedy. (You may think otherwise, as you are my beneficiary—but don't worry, I don't have millions.) But, seriously, that money needs to be shared. It needs to be given to our world and to other people. Find something: a cause, your church, a health organization, or a local family.

I pray this book has brought you knowledge and skills that will help you on the road as you begin your journey. As a parent, my deepest desire is for you to be healthy, happy and safe. I also want you prepared to stand on your own two feet, so that you will experience independence and confidence. The money skills taught in this book will be instrumental as you venture out.

I heard a quote a long time ago while on a teleconference. I loved it and it has always stuck with me. (Unfortunately, I don't know who originally said it.) Here is that quote: "There are two great moments in your life. One is when you were born and the other is when you figure out *why*." Go figure out why, baby. It will be one of the happiest days of your life.

About the Author

Although Patti Handy has extensive work experience in the banking and mortgage world, she attributes most of her "money smarts" to her life experiences. Her parents taught her at a very young age how to respect and manage money. As a result of this solid foundation at a young age, she has been able to not only survive some of life's challenges, but thrive through them.

When her son was just eighteen months old, Patti went through a divorce that turned her world upside down. Not wanting to put her son in daycare after the divorce, she chose not to go back to corporate America, where she had spent many years. As a result of time away from a regular paycheck and the financial strains of a divorce, she found herself drained—emotionally, physically, and financially.

With the *money sense* foundation she had from childhood, financial skills she learned "on the job," and strength she gained through her faith, she was able to pull herself out from under the mess and debt. She not only managed to keep her home, she then went on to purchase additional investment properties and invest in the stock market.

As a result of these life experiences (and a few others), she has made it her mission to educate and empower teens with the same money smarts she gained so young. Realizing this foundation set the stage for her success later in life, she is passionate about reaching out to share this gift.

A bit more information from a purely educational and work experience perspective: After receiving her bachelor's degree in accounting, Patti spent a combined twenty-five years in the banking and mortgage world. While working in banking, she obtained her Series 7 and 63 licenses, which she held for ten years. Most recently, she has been a Senior Mortgage Advisor for over seven years, presently holding a real estate brokers license, and is a CTA Certified Life Coach.

Got questions for Patti?
Go to www.teenscashcoach.com and sign
up for the free weekly video series,
"The Money Minute."

You can submit your questions via email
and she will respond on her weekly video!

Email her directly at
support@teenscashcoach.com

Bring Patti to you with *The Prosperous
Teen*™, a DVD program and workbook,
which covers the information in this book
and much more!
Visit www.teenscashcoach.com and click on
"Products" to learn more.

Notes and Action Steps

Notes and Action Steps

Notes and Action Steps

Notes and Action Steps

Notes and Action Steps

Notes and Action Steps

Notes and Action Steps

Notes and Action Steps

_____

_____

_____

_____

_____

_____

_____

_____

_____

_____

_____

_____

_____

_____

_____

_____

_____

_____

_____

_____

_____

_____

_____

_____

_____

_____

Notes and Action Steps